THE ONE WAY

for 11 - 14s

BOOK 2

CHRISTIAN FOCUS PUBLICATIONS

We believe that the Bible is God's word to mankind, and that it contains everything we need to know in order to be reconciled with God and live in a way that is pleasing to him. Therefore, we believe it is vital to teach young teens accurately from the Bible, being careful to teach each passage's true meaning in an appropriate way for the age group, rather than selecting a 'teen's message' from a Biblical passage.

© TnT Ministries
29 Buxton Gardens, Acton, London, W3 9LE
Tel: +44 (0)20 8992 0450 Fax: +44 (0)20 8896 1847
e-mail: sales@tntministries.org.uk

Published in 2002 by Christian Focus Publications Ltd.
Geanies House, Fearn, Tain, Ross-shire, IV20 1TW
Tel: +44 (0)1862 871 011 Fax: +44 (0)1862 871 699
e-mail: **info@christianfocus.com**
www.christianfocus.com

Cover design by Profile Designs

This book and others in the series can be purchased from your local Christian bookshop. Alternatively you can write to TnT Ministries direct or place your order with the publisher.

ISBN- 1-85792-705-2

TnT Ministries (which stands for Teaching and Training Ministries) was launched in February 1993 by Christians from a broad variety of denominational backgrounds who were concerned that teaching the Bible to children be taken seriously. The leaders were in charge of the Sunday School of 50 teachers at St Helen's Bishopsgate, an evangelical church in the City of London, for 13 years, during which time a range of Biblical teaching materials was developed. TnT Ministries also runs training days for Sunday School teachers.

CONTENTS

On the Way for 11-14s / Book 2

Contributors

Preparation of Bible material:
Wendy Barber
Thalia Blundell
Annie Gemmill

Editing:
David Jackman

Activities & Puzzles:
Wendy Barber
Thalia Blundell
Rachel Garforth-Bles
Jennefer Lord
Nick Margesson

On The Way for 11-14s works on a 3 year syllabus consisting of 6 books. It builds on the 9-11s syllabus and introduces young teens to study the Bible in a way which is challenging and intellectually stretching. Because they are often unprepared to take things at face value and are encouraged to question everything, it is important to satisfy the mind while touching the heart. Therefore, some of the lessons are designed to introduce the idea of further Bible study skills, e.g. the use of a concordance, a character study, studying a single verse or a passage.

Lessons are grouped in series, each of which is introduced by a series overview stating the aims of the series, the lesson aim for each week, and an appropriate memory verse. Every lesson, in addition to an aim, has study notes to enable the teacher to understand the Bible passage, a suggestion to focus attention on the study to follow, a 'Question Section' and an activity for the group to do. The Question Section consists of 2-3 questions designed to help in discussing the application of the Bible passage. The course can be joined at any time during its 3 year cycle.

To prepare a Sunday School lesson properly takes at least one evening (2-3 hours). It is helpful to read the Bible passage several days before teaching it to allow time to mull over what it is saying.

When preparing a lesson the following steps should be taken -

1. PRAY!

In a busy world this is very easy to forget. We are unable to understand God's word without his help and we need to remind ourselves of that fact before we start.

2. READ THE BIBLE PASSAGE

This should be done *before* reading the lesson manual. Our resource is the Bible, not what someone says about it. The Bible study notes in the lesson manual are a commentary on the passage to help you understand it.

3. LOOK AT THE LESSON AIM

This should reflect the main teaching of the passage. Plan how that can be packaged appropriately for the age group you teach.

4. TEACHING THE BIBLE PASSAGE

This should take place in the context of simple Bible study. Do ensure that the children use the same version of the Bible. Prior to the lesson decide how the passage will be read, (e.g. one verse at a time), and who should do the reading. Is the passage short enough to read the whole of it or should some parts be paraphrased by the teacher? Work through the passage, deciding which points should be raised. Design simple questions to bring out the main teaching of the passage. The first questions should elicit the facts and should be designed so that they cannot be answered by a simple 'no' or 'yes'. If a group member reads out a Bible verse as the answer, praise him/her and then ask him/her to put it in his/her own words. Once the facts have been established go on to application questions, encouraging the group to think through how the teaching can be applied to their lives. The 'Question Section' is designed to help you when it comes to discussing the application of the Bible passage.

5. VISUAL AIDS

Pictures are very rarely required for this age group. A Bible Timeline is useful so that the young people can see where the Bible passage they are studying comes in the big picture of God's revelation to his people. You can find one at the back of this book. A map is helpful to demonstrate distances, etc. A flip chart or similar is handy to summarise the lesson.

6. ACTIVITIES AND PUZZLES

These are designed to reinforce the Bible teaching and very little prior preparation (if any) is required by the teacher.

• Encourages the leaders to study the Bible for themselves.

• Teaches young people Bible-study skills.

• Everything you need is in the one book, so there is no need to buy activity books.

• Undated materials allow you to use the lessons to fit your situation without wasting materials.

• Once you have the entire syllabus, there is no need to repurchase.

On The Way for 11-14s is designed to teach young teens how to read and understand a passage of Scripture and then apply it to their lives (see How to Prepare a Lesson). Before learning how to study the Bible they need to know what it is and how to find their way around it.

The Bible

Christians believe that the Bible is God's word and contains all we need to know in order to live in relationship with God and with each other. It is the way God has chosen to reveal himself to mankind; it not only records historical facts but also interprets those facts. It is not a scientific text book.

What does the Bible consist of?

The Bible is God's story. It is divided into 2 sections - the Old and New Testaments. 'Testament' means 'covenant' or 'promise'.

The Old Testament contains 39 books covering the period from creation to about 400 years before the birth of Jesus. It records God's mighty acts of creation, judgment and mercy as well as their interpretation through the words of the prophets.

The New Testament is made up of 27 books containing details of the life, death and resurrection of Jesus, the spread of the gospel in the early Church, Christian doctrine and the final judgment.

Who wrote the Bible?

The books of the Bible were written by many different people, some known and others not. Christians believe that all these authors were inspired by God (2 Peter 1:20-21, 2 Timothy 3:16). As a result we can trust what it says.

How can we find our way around it?

Each book in the Bible is divided into chapters, each one of which contains a number of verses. When the Books were written originally the chapter and verse divisions were absent. These have been added to enable the readers to find their way around. When written down they are recorded in the following way, Genesis 5:1-10. This tells us to look up the book of Genesis, chapter 5, verses 1 to 10.

At the front of the Bible is a contents page, listing the books in the order in which they come in the Bible. It is perfectly acceptable to look up the index to see which page to turn to.

Aids to teach the Bible passage

- Many of the lessons have activity pages that help to bring out the main teaching of the Bible passage.
- Packs of maps and charts can be purchased from Christian book shops.
- A Bible Time Line is useful to reinforce the chronology of the Bible (see back of this book).

Questions to aid in understanding

Periodically use the following questions to help the young people understand the passage:
- Who wrote it?
- To whom was it written?
- When was it written?
- What situation is being described? (if applicable)

To make a chart of the Bible Library enlarge the template below and photocopy as required. Draw 2 sets of shelves on a large piece of paper (see diagram). Label the shelves. Cut off the unwanted books from each set and write the names of the books on the spines. Glue the books onto the appropriate shelves in the order in which they appear in the Bible.

The Bible Library

Old Testament	New Testament
Law (5 books)	Gospels & Acts (5)
History (12 books)	Paul's Epistles (13)
Poetry & Wisdom (5)	Other Epistles (8)
Prophets (17 books)	Prophecy (1 book)

OVERVIEW
Rescue

Week 1   **The Passover**   *Exodus 12:1-28*
To see how the Passover points forwards to God's plan of salvation through Jesus.

Week 2   **The Day of Atonement**   *Leviticus 16:1-34*
To understand that sin has to be dealt with before we can worship a holy God.

Week 3   **The New Covenant**   *Hebrews 9:1-28*
To understand why Jesus' death makes it possible for us to approach a holy God.

SERIES AIMS

To understand how the Passover and the rituals enacted on the Day of Atonement help explain Jesus' death on the cross.

MEMORY WORK

Without the shedding of blood there is no forgiveness.

Hebrews 9:22

Rescue

When God made the first man, Adam, he chose to have a friendship with him. God talked with him, revealed himself to him, gave him a job to do and gave him a rule to keep. When Adam and Eve rebelled against God, breaking the rule that God had given them, they became sinful. Since God is perfect he could not live in fellowship with them anymore and he banished them from his presence (the garden). All the children descended from Adam and Eve were born rebels. No-one was fit to live with God.

Later in the book of Genesis we read about something very remarkable. God made a promise to Abraham, an ordinary sinful man, one not fit to be in his presence. God promised that Abraham and his descendants would be God's special people and he would be their God. Could it be that God was prepared to ignore Abraham's sinful nature in order to be friends with him? **NO**, we know that God **cannot** do that. So how **could** a holy God make that promise to a sinful man?

About 450 years later the descendants of Abraham's grandson, Jacob (later named Israel), became slaves in the land of Egypt. Because of his promise to Abraham, God rescued the Israelites and led them out of Egypt into the desert. There he showed Moses how the Israelites should behave as God's people. He also showed them how he would arrange things so that a holy God could live among them despite their sin.

In this series we will be looking at the way God rescued his people from Egypt (the Passover) and the instructions for worship that were given to Moses regarding the Day of Atonement. We will see that worship was not something a person decided to do for God. When people worshipped God they were following the instructions that God had given them! In this way God could accept them as his people, despite their sinfulness, and live among them as their God. The last study looks at the way Jesus Christ completely fulfilled the requirements of the Law. Through his death we have not only been redeemed but are free to enter God's presence and live in fellowship with him.

PREPARATION

Exodus 12:1-28,
Matthew 26:17-30

LESSON AIMS

To see how the Passover points forward to God's plan of salvation through Jesus.

This study looks at the institution of the Passover. The Passover Feast was linked with the Feast of Unleavened Bread (Leviticus 23:5-6) and was the time when the Jewish people remembered their deliverance from Egypt.

During the months of the plagues Pharaoh had been given every opportunity to repent of his arrogance and acknowledge God, but had refused. This refusal caused judgment to fall on the entire nation of Egypt. Unlike the other plagues, when God had used natural phenomena in supernatural ways, the death of the first-born was by direct intervention. Moses and Aaron were not told to call up this plague - God stated the time and way he was to act. In order to escape, the Israelites had to follow the specific instructions God gave to Moses.

The group needs to look at how the Passover foreshadows Christ's death (John 1:29, 1 Corinthians 5:7) - the lamb had to be male, without defects, and its blood had to be shed and applied to the house; the people had to remain within the house if the blood was to be effective. By the time of Jesus, (about 1300 years later), the Passover lambs were killed in the Temple in Jerusalem and the blood was poured out onto the sides of the altar. The lambs were eaten as a kind of fellowship offering. At the Last Supper Jesus, by talking about **his** blood being poured out (Matthew 26:27-28), was telling his disciples that he was going to be a sacrifice like the Passover lamb. The blood of the Passover lamb was propitiatory, turning away God's wrath, so its sacrifice had a redemptive ingredient as well as bringing about the rescue of God's people from slavery in Egypt. Jesus' death rescues people from their sinfulness and enables them to live in fellowship with God.

Exodus

12:2   Previously the Jewish year had begun in what is our September. From that time on it was to start in our mid-March. The Jewish religious year still starts at this point. Note that God gave Moses instructions for remembering the Passover **before** the death of the first-born took place. There was no doubt in Moses' mind that God would rescue his people in the way he had determined.

12:5   The lamb had to be male and without defect.

12:8   Bread baked without the yeast - i.e. baked in haste.

12:11   Shoes were not normally worn inside.

Matthew

26:17   The lambs were ritually slaughtered in the temple precincts and the meal took place in any house within the city bounds and in small companies. It was only following the destruction of the Temple in AD 70 that the ceremony reverted to a domestic one.

26:19   Preparation included checking that no leaven was present, providing a basin and towel for hand washing, and preparing the lamb, bitter herbs, unleavened bread and 4 cups of wine.

26:20   The Passover Meal. Before the meal ritual hand washing was strictly observed. The meal consisted of roast lamb, bitter herbs, unleavened bread, and 4 cups of wine at specified points. Prior to the 2nd cup of wine all the food was cleared from the table and the story of the Exodus was recounted as a dialogue between father and son (or suitable substitutes). The food was then brought back and part of the Hallel (Pss.113-118) was sung. This was followed by the 2nd cup of wine. Then came the breaking of the bread. (This was probably the point when Judas received his sop and disappeared, John 13:30.) This was followed by the 3rd cup of wine. The singing of the Hallel was then completed and the 4th cup of wine drunk (26:30).

Originally the meal was eaten standing, dressed ready for a journey (Exodus 12:11). That custom had been abandoned as a sign that the Jews were no longer slaves but free.

26:26   Jesus uses the bread to point forward to his coming death; in the Passover meal it was normally used to point backwards to the Exodus.

26:27   The 3rd cup of wine. For the new covenant see Jeremiah 31:31-34.

1. What are the similarities between the Passover story and Jesus' death on the cross?

2. What other Old Testament stories do you know that are pictures of salvation? (Genesis 6-9; 22:1-19; 37-46, Exodus 13:17 - 14:31, Ruth 1-4)

Pointing Forward   Clear space in the middle of the room and ask for a volunteer. The volunteer stands in the centre of the space and places a broom on their forehead, standing upright. Looking up towards the head of the broom, the person spins round 20 times, with the rest of the group counting. After 20 turns the person has to drop the broom and try to point forward. (Needless to say, the results are often hilarious.) Repeat with other volunteers as time allows.

Use this activity to introduce the idea of pointing forward. Today's Bible passage also points forward. Can you work out what to?

Photocopy page 11 for each group member. The Bible verse is Hebrews 9:22.

If time permits celebrate a simplified Passover meal. The time required is 15-20 minutes.

Each small group requires:

- 1 candle plus matches
- 3 pieces of unleavened bread (Matzot, or pitta bread if Matzot unobtainable), placed one on top of another, separated by paper napkins
- Bitter herbs - use watercress or flat leafed parsley
- Small bunch of parsley and bowl of salt water
- Charoset - use applesauce mixed with cinnamon and raisins. It represents the mortar used in slavery in Egypt.
- Roast lamb (obtainable pre-packed from some supermarkets)
- 4 cups of wine - use red juice.
- Plastic plates, napkins, paper cup.

Sit in groups of 10-12 in a circle, with the candle in the centre. The leader's comments are in italic.

1. Recall the search for leaven and its removal.

2. Light the candle.

    Blessed are you, Lord God, who created light.

3. Fill the cup with red juice (first cup).

    God said: 'I will bring you out from under the burdens of the Egyptians.' Blessed are you, Lord God, King of the universe.

    Pass round the cup.

4. Dip parsley in the bowl of salt water.

    Remember the hyssop dipped in the blood of the lamb, which was painted on the lintel and doorposts.

5. Break the middle matzah in half and put half to one side on a napkin. Hold up the other half.

    This is the bread of affliction, which our fathers ate in the land of Egypt.

    Replace with other 2 matzot.

6. Fill the cup with red juice (second cup).

    God said: 'I will deliver you from out of their bondage.'

7. Youngest present asks -

    Why is this night different from all other nights?

    Reply - *We were slaves to Pharaoh in Egypt, and the Lord our God brought us out with a mighty hand and an outstretched arm. If God had not brought us out we would still be Pharaoh's slaves.*

8. Point to the various items on the table.

   What is the meaning of the lamb? It is the sacrifice of the Lord's Passover when he passed over our houses and slew the Egyptians.

   What is the meaning of the unleavened bread? Our fathers baked unleavened bread because they were thrust out of Egypt and could not wait.

   What is the meaning of the bitter herbs? The Egyptians made our fathers' lives bitter with all kinds of hard work.

9. Raise the second cup of red juice.

   We thank you, O Lord, for delivering us from bondage.

   Pass round the cup.

10. Break the upper and middle half matzah into the required number of portions for each person in the group.

   Bless you, O Lord our God, King of the universe.

Pass round.

11. Pick up bitter herbs and charoset.

   Blessed are you, O Lord our God, King of the universe.

   Dip watercress into the charoset, passing from person to person.

12. Break the lower matzah into the required number of portions and distribute with the remaining watercress. Pass round the lamb.

13. Break the remaining half matzah and distribute.

14. Fill the cup with red juice (third cup).

   God said: 'I will redeem you with an outstretched arm'. Blessed are you, O Lord our God, King of the universe.

   Pass round the cup.

15. Fill the cup with red juice (fourth cup).

   God said: 'I will take you to me for a people'. Thank you, Lord God, that you are our King and our Saviour.

   Pass round the cup.

16. *The remembrance of the Passover is now complete.*

Fit the jigsaw pieces into the grid to discover an important stattement. There are no gaps between the words and the shaded squares in the jigsaw pieces correspond to the shaded squares in the grid.

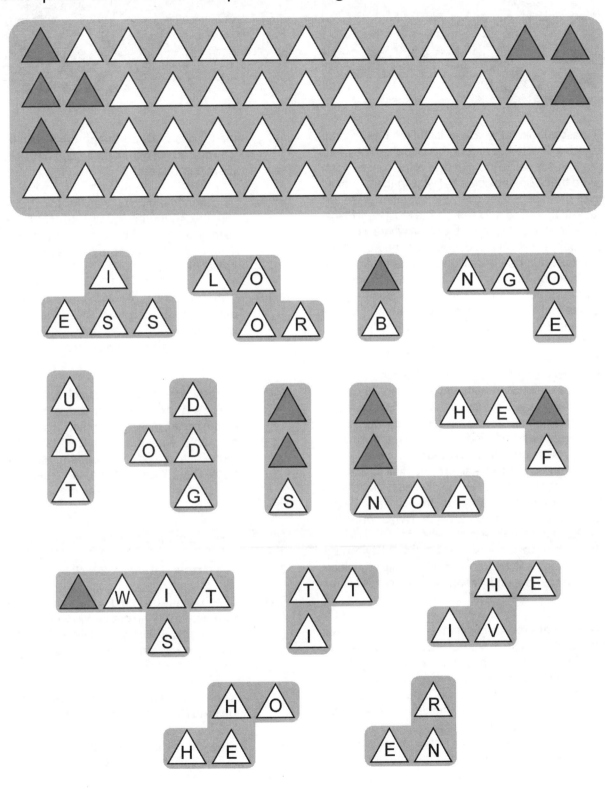

The text is from Hebrews chapter 9. Which verse is it?

PREPARATION

Leviticus 16:1-34

LESSON AIMS

To understand that sin has to be dealt with before we can worship a holy God.

This lesson looks at what the Israelites had to do if God was going to live among his people. They had the Tabernacle set up in the middle of the camp, which showed that God had come to live with them, just as he had promised. However, the Israelites were still not able to be in God's presence. The Most Holy Place, with the Ark of the Covenant, the place where a person could really meet with God, was screened off with a big curtain. No-one was allowed in, apart from the High Priest on the Day of Atonement. On the one hand the Tabernacle seemed to be teaching the Israelites that God could now live with them, on the other hand the curtain acted as a huge 'no entry' sign.

So we are faced with the big problem, how can a holy God live with sinful people? In the book of Leviticus we read the instructions God gave to Moses about the various things the Israelites had to do if God was to live among them, including the various sacrifices. If a sinful man came before God, God's anger at that man's sin would be so great that he could not survive. When a person brought an animal as a sacrifice to God, he laid his hand on its head. As he did this his sins were symbolically transferred onto the animal. What happened to the animal after that was what the **worshipper** deserved because of his sin. This enabled the worshipper to come near to God without dying as a result. Anyone watching an animal being killed instead of them would have understood the seriousness of their sin.

It seemed that even the constant sacrifices of animals on people's behalf could not stop the Tabernacle becoming tarnished with their sin, so, once a year on the Day of Atonement, the High Priest had to carry out a special ceremony to make the Tabernacle and the people as a whole clean again. Atonement is the action of bringing together two people or groups of people who are enemies and enabling them to be friends. In the Bible this usually means doing something about sin.

16:1   Aaron and his sons, Abihu and Nadab, had been consecrated priests (Leviticus 8). Then the 2 sons decided to approach God in a way he had not commanded and were killed (Leviticus 10:1-3).

16:2   The atonement cover was the lid of the ark with the 2 cherubim on its top. It indicated mercy as well as holiness. Even the High Priest could only approach God in the prescribed manner.

16:3-5   The total number of animals required were 1 bull, 2 rams and 2 goats. The bull and 1 ram were offered on behalf of the High Priest, the remaining animals were offered on behalf of the people.

16:4   Note the simplicity of the clothing. The High Priest's normal clothing was elaborately embroidered, making him magnificent to look at. This was suitable for his role of representing God to the people. However, on the Day of Atonement he was representing the people to God, so was dressed like a slave.

16:6-10   This is a summary of the day's rituals.

16:8   The scapegoat - see v.20-22.

16:11-22   These verses go into detail about the rituals summarised in the preceding verses. Note that God gave very specific instructions about the way sin was to be dealt with. The people were not allowed to choose their own way to God. In the same way today, there is only one mediator between God and men, the man Christ Jesus (1 Timothy 2:5).

16:11   Before the High Priest can deal with the people's sin he must deal with his own.

16:13   This verse seems to suggest that if the High Priest looked on the atonement cover he would die. By the time of Jesus the High

Priest went into the Most Holy Place with a rope tied round his ankle so that if he was struck dead he could be pulled out again.

16:16   This verse probably refers to the articles of furniture in the tent rather than the tent itself (cf. Hebrews 9:21-22).

16:17   Note that Aaron had to do this all on his own. He was the only mediator.

16:20-22   The High Priest confessed all the wickedness and rebellion of the people over the scapegoat's head. Instead of sacrificing the goat, it was taken into the desert and left there. The scapegoat took the people's sin away from the camp, never to return. The New Testament never uses the scapegoat as a picture of Jesus. However, 2 Corinthians 5:21 and 1 Peter 2:24 speak of Jesus being made sin on our behalf and bearing our sins, which are similar to the scapegoat.

16:23-28   These verses speak of the rituals required following the sacrifices and sending away of the scapegoat.

16:23-24   Note the importance of washing both before and after (cf. v.4). Cleansing was required after any contact with sin (see also v.26,28).

16:24   It was only after sin had been dealt with that the burnt offerings could be sacrificed. The burnt offerings were a way of saying thank-you to God (see Leviticus 1:1-17).

16:29-34   These verses deal with the date and what is required from the people. Note that it was to be a lasting ordinance - there would never come a time when people could deal with their own sin.

Next week we will study the passage in Hebrews which shows how the Day of Atonement pointed forwards to Jesus' death on the cross.

 QUESTIONS

1. What do we learn about God's view of sin from the rituals enacted on the Day of Atonement?

2. When Jesus died on the cross he paid the penalty for sin (John 3:16). God has promised to forgive everyone who turns to him in repentance (1 John 1:9) so does it matter if we sin? (see Romans 6:11-15)

3. How can we help each other in the war against sin?

FOCUS ACTIVITY

Arch Enemies   On self-adhesive labels write down famous pairs of arch enemies or rivals (one name per label).

Suggested pairs:
Tom & Jerry
Winston Churchil & Adolf Hitler
Arsenal & Tottenham Hotspur (football teams)
Batman & The Penguin
Live and Kicking & SMTV Live (television programmes)
Sherlock Holmes & Professor Moriarty
Road Runner & Wile E Coyote.

Stick one label on the back of each person in the group without them seeing who they are. The object of the exercise is for each person to find out who they are and pair up with their arch enemy by only asking questions with the answer 'yes' or 'no'. The losers are the last two people to find each other.

Is this a good way of bringing enemies together? Let's see how God solved the problem in the Old Testament.

ACTIVITY

Photocopy page 14 for each group member.

In the following word square are hidden 2 names, 4 animals, 15 nouns, 1 number and 2 verbs, all taken from today's Bible passage. Each word runs horizontally and vertically and can change direction any number of times. The first word is shown for you. All the letters are used. No letter is used more than once. At the end of each word an arrow indicates where the next word starts.

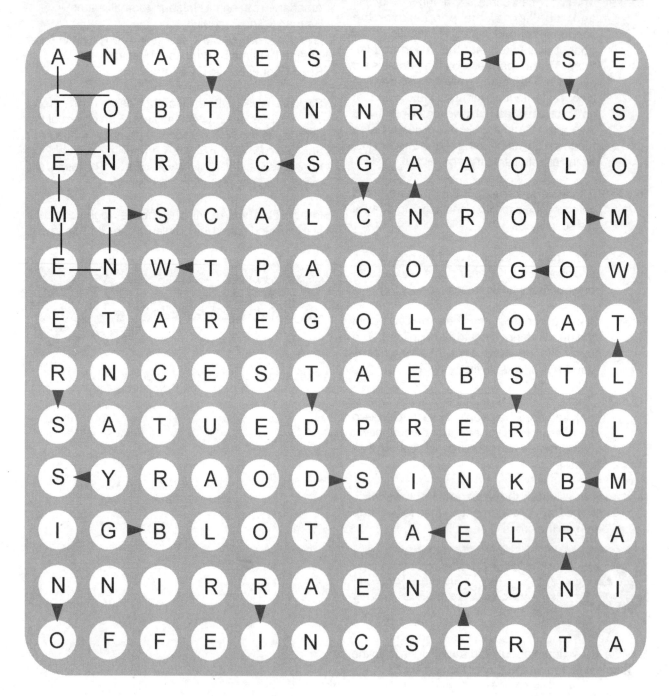

PREPARATION

Hebrews 9:1-28

LESSON AIMS

To understand why Jesus' death makes it possible for us to approach a holy God.

When God met with Moses on Mount Sinai he made a covenant with the Israelites. God promised that he would be their God and they would be his people. They had to keep his commandments, build the Tabernacle and perform sacrifices so that they could have their sins forgiven. However, there were 3 main problems. The Israelites could not go into God's presence - if they did they would die. The temple curtain made this very clear to the people. The second problem was the problem of sin. In spite of the daily sacrifices the people's sins remained. The third problem was the inability of the people to keep their side of the agreement.

9:1   This refers to the covenant made at Mount Sinai. The author deals with 2 aspects - the tabernacle and the regulations for worship.

9:2-5   The tabernacle was an earthly sanctuary (v.1), which limited its ability to promote a relationship with God. It was made with human hands, but was a picture of what was to come (v.11-12).

9:3   The curtain separated the Most Holy Place from the Holy Place. The atonement cover with its 2 gold cherubim symbolised God's presence (Exodus 25:17-22). The curtain was a vivid picture of the people's inability to enter the presence of a holy God (problem 1).

9:3-4   According to Exodus 30:1-7, the altar of incense was in the Holy Place, not the Most Holy Place. This is borne out by the command to burn incense on the altar every day and every night (Exodus 30:8-9), as the only time the Most Holy Place was entered was by the High Priest once a year on the Day of Atonement (v.7, cf. Leviticus 16:1-2, 34).

9:4   Initially the ark contained the stone tablets God gave to Moses at Mount Sinai (Exodus

25:16; 40:20). At some stage the jar of manna (Exodus 16:33-34) and Aaron's rod (Numbers 17:8-11) were added.

9:5   The atonement cover was where the blood was sprinkled on the Day of Atonement (Leviticus 16:14-16).

9:6-10 This section deals with the second aspect of the old covenant, the regulations for worship.

9:6   The people were dependent on the ministry of the priests, they could not approach God themselves.

9:7   Cf. v.22.

9:8   In this context the first tabernacle seems to imply the whole system of worship, not just the tent.

9:9   In spite of the system of sacrifices, the people's sins still remained (problem 2). The people were unable to keep their side of the covenant (problem 3), but continuously rebelled against God (Hebrews 8:9).

9:9-10 The old covenant with its sacrifices would only apply until the time of the new covenant. God's new covenant was not made because the old one had gone wrong. It was always God's intention to restore the relationship that Adam had broken, by sending his son into this world to die on behalf of sinful people.

9:11-28 These verses deal with the new covenant. Having dealt with the earthly sanctuary and its regulations for worship in the preceding verses, the writer now turns to the heavenly sanctuary and its regulations for worship.

9:11   Jesus, as our High Priest, has gone into the heavenly Most Holy Place. By speaking of

Jesus being the 'high priest of the good things that are already here', the writer is pointing out that the things foreshadowed in the OT have now arrived. The imagery of Jesus passing through into the Most Holy Place is taken from the Day of Atonement (Leviticus 16).

9:12   Not only is Jesus the High Priest, he is also the sacrifice. Jesus entered the Most Holy Place (heaven) once for all, unlike the High Priest who went in every year. Also, the redemption Jesus obtained for us is eternal, not something which has to be repurchased by continuing sacrifices.

9:13-14   Jesus' death is the answer to problem 2. Note that we are sanctified in order to serve. This was also true of the rituals of the Old Covenant.

9:15   Under the Old Covenant the inheritance was the land of Canaan. Under the New Covenant the inheritance is heaven. Note that there is only one mediator, in the same way that the High Priest was the only mediator on the Day of Atonement.

Jesus' death is retrospective - it deals with all the sins committed under the Old Covenant.

By ushering in the New Covenant Jesus deals with problem 3. The New Covenant brought a real change in people's hearts (Jeremiah 31:31-34, Hebrews 8:10-11). Although forgiven people are not perfect they **want** to obey God. When we get to heaven we will be able to obey God perfectly!

9:16   The word used for 'will' is the same Greek word used for 'covenant'.

9:18   The covenant maker did not die to effect the first covenant, but blood still needed to be shed, so an animal died instead.

9:19-20   See Exodus 24:1-8.

9:21   See Leviticus 8:15; 16:15-19.

9:22   Although this is talking about ceremonial cleansing (cf. v.13) it is also pointing towards the people's need to be freed from the penalty of sin.

9:23   The writer is not suggesting that heaven contained sin and so needed cleansing through Christ's sacrifice. It may be that he was suggesting that Jesus' sacrifice had an effect on the whole of creation (cf. Romans 8:20-21).

9:24   Jesus is in heaven, appearing for us in God's presence. This answers problem 1.

9:26-28   Jesus' death is a sufficient sacrifice for the sins of everyone throughout the whole of time.

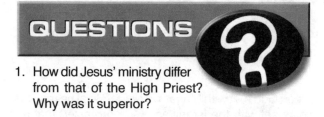

QUESTIONS

1. How did Jesus' ministry differ from that of the High Priest? Why was it superior?

2. Why was Jesus' death a better sacrifice than those offered under the Old Covenant? How did it deal with the problem of sin?

FOCUS ACTIVITY

Keep Away
Get the group members to form a circle holding hands. One person stands in the middle of the circle. The object of the game is to pull other people onto the person standing in the middle. As soon as someone touches the person in the middle they are out. They drop out of the circle, which reforms and the game continues. The winner is the person left at the end who has successfully avoided touching the person in the middle.

Use the activity to introduce the idea of someone being unapproachable. Remind the group of the previous week's lesson and the problem of how a holy God could live among sinful people. Let's see how that problem was dealt with once and for all.

A quiz to revise the series. Divide the group into 2 teams. The winner is the first team to collect 6 unblemished sheep (see diagram).

Requirements

Each team requires a set of 8 sheep, 6 unmarked and 2 with marks to indicate blemishes. The sheep are randomly numbered from 1-8 on the back and are pinned to the board with the numbers showing. The blemished sheep introduce an element of chance so that a team member who answers a question incorrectly will not place their team in an irretrievable position. Prepare 16 questions to bring out the main points from the series.

Rules

A question is put to each team in turn and, if answered correctly, one of the team members chooses a sheep by calling out its number. The sheep is turned over and, if unblemished, is left on the board. A blemished sheep is removed from the board. If an incorrect answer is given the question is offered to the other team. Allow 10 minutes for the quiz.

OVERVIEW
Paul and the Gospel

Week 4

Conversion   *Acts 7:54 - 8:3; 9:1-30, Galatians 1:13-24*
To understand that conversion results in a changed life.

Week 5

Commission   *Acts 13:1-12*
To understand how Paul and Barnabas were commissioned for service.

Week 6

Preaching the Gospel   *Acts 13:13-52*
To learn the principles of presenting the gospel.

Week 7

Opposition to the Gospel   *Acts 14:1-28*
To understand that preaching the gospel brings opposition.

Week 8

The Sufficiency of the Gospel   *Acts 15:1-35*
To distinguish between God's laws made for all time and those that were given for a particular period.

Week 9

The Servant of the Gospel   *Acts 15:36 - 16:15*
To learn what qualities should be demonstrated in the life of the Christian.

Week 10

Suffering for the Gospel   *Acts 16:16-40*
To understand how a Christian should react when punished unjustly.

SERIES AIMS

1. To see God's plan of salvation extending from the Jews to the Gentiles and into Europe.

2. Through Paul's life and work to learn about the early church.

MEMORY WORK

God disciplines us for our good, that we may share in his holiness.

Hebrews 12:10

Paul and the Gospel

Paul was born in Tarsus and was, therefore, a Roman citizen. He was a Jew from the tribe of Benjamin and became a zealous member of the party of the Pharisees. His credentials as a Jew were highly commendable (Philippians 3:5-6). He was taught by Gamaliel, the most honoured Rabbi of the 1st Century (Acts 22:3). As a young man Paul approved the stoning of Stephen (Acts 7:57 - 8:3) and was given official permission to persecute the emerging Christian church (Acts 9:1-2). His education and early rise to fame would suggest that his family was quite wealthy and influential; his nephew's access to the Jerusalem leaders adds weight to this idea (Acts 23:16-22).

After Paul's conversion on the road to Damascus the Lord said of him, 'This is my chosen instrument to carry my name before the Gentiles and their kings and before the people of Israel. I will show him how much he must suffer for my name.' (Acts 9:15-16). All this came true, as we shall see in the following weeks.

Following his conversion, Paul spent some time in the desert then returned to Damascus, a total of 3 years (Galatians 1:15-18). Due to persecution from the Jews he fled to Jerusalem, where he was initially shunned by the apostles until Barnabas introduced him to them and explained what had happened (Acts 9:23-27). Two weeks later Paul was again forced to flee for his life. He went to his home town of Tarsus, where he stayed for 10 years (Acts 9:29-30, Galatians 1:18-21). Barnabas, hearing of Paul's work, requested him to come to Antioch to help in the flourishing Gentile mission there (Acts 11:19-26). After a year of notable blessing, the church at Antioch sent Paul and Barnabas with gifts for the famine stricken church in Jerusalem (Acts 11:27-30).

In approximately AD 46, upon their return from Jerusalem, the church at Antioch commissioned Paul and Barnabas to evangelise, as instructed by the Holy Spirit (Acts 13:1-3), and so began a series of missionary enterprises.

The pattern established by the 2 evangelists was to preach first in the synagogues to give the Jews and God-fearing Gentiles the chance to hear the gospel message. Only when the Jews rejected the gospel, often with violence, did Paul turn his attention to the Gentiles. Despite many difficulties, including the defection of John Mark, the mission to Galatia succeeded in establishing churches in Pisidian Antioch, Iconium, Lystra, Derbe and possibly Perga.

The number of Gentiles becoming Christians posed a serious threat to the Jewish Christians, some of whom insisted that the new converts should be circumcised and subject to the Mosaic Law. In AD 49, on their return to Antioch from Galatia, Paul and Barnabas opposed this teaching. The church sent them up to Jerusalem to meet with the apostles to sort out the problem (Acts 15:1-2). At this Council meeting the apostles listened to Paul's account of the wonderful things God had done for the Gentiles. Then they decided that circumcision was not necessary for salvation, but the Gentile converts should abstain from sexual immorality and meat sacrificed to idols (Acts 15:12-20).

From Antioch Paul set out on his second missionary journey, accompanied by Silas due to a disagreement with Barnabas about John Mark (Acts 15:36-41). They travelled overland through Syria and Cilicia visiting the churches on their way. At Lystra Timothy joined them (Acts 16:1-3). Forbidden by the Holy Spirit to go west into Asia, they went into Northern Galatia and from there across to Greece and established the Macedonian churches of Philippi, Thessalonica and Berea.

This series ends with Paul in Philippi and is followed by a 5 week series on Paul's Epistle to the Philippians. The remainder of Paul's second missionary journey will be studied after the series on Philippians and Paul's third missionary journey will be looked at in Book 4.

PREPARATION

Acts 7:54 - 8:3;
9:1-30,
Galatians 1:13-24

LESSON AIMS

To understand that conversion results in a changed life.

In Acts Luke records the lengths Saul went to in persecuting the church; he was known as a hater of Christians. The passages in Acts give a clear idea of Saul before his conversion, and Paul after his experience of God's intervention. Galatians is interesting as it shows Paul's theological background and underlines the remarkable change in Paul's life.

Acts

7:54 This follows the sermon Stephen had just preached in which he stated that the Jews had killed Jesus, the Righteous One.

7:57 Where the Gospel is preached opposition follows, cf. John 3:19.

7:58 Saul was probably in charge of Stephen's execution.

8:1 Luke shows clearly how Saul felt about Christianity - this is the first Biblical account of Saul's character.

In spite of the persecution in Jerusalem the apostles stayed on whilst the other disciples scattered. It would encourage the infant church to know that the apostles were not running away from persecution.

8:3 Note the extent of Saul's hatred.

9:1 'Murderous threats' - we know of his consent to Stephen's murder, and there may well have been other deaths.

9:2 Damascus was in Syria, a Roman province. It was the nearest important city outside Palestine with a large Jewish population. For Saul and the Sanhedrin it was important to stop the new 'Way' spreading from Damascus, which was a key trading centre. From here trade routes radiated out to Syria, Mesopotamia, Anatolia, Persia and Arabia. Saul would want to bring back prisoners to Jerusalem where they would be tried by the Sanhedrin.

9:4 'Persecute me' - those who persecute Christians persecute Jesus.

9:11 Straight Street was a colonnaded street approximately a mile in length, which bisected Roman Damascus.

9:13,32 'Saints'. All Christians are 'saints' in the Biblical sense of the word, i.e. set apart to God and being made increasingly more holy by the work of the Holy Spirit.

9:15 The first mention of Paul's God-given calling as an apostle to the Gentiles.

9:17 Jesus himself actually appeared, not merely a vision. This experience qualified him as an apostle (1 Corinthians 9:1; 15:8).

9:23 'Many days' is 3 years, as is seen in Galatians 1:17-18. Probably most of this time was spent in Arabia, away from Damascus, but he returned there.

9:27 Barnabas (see 4:36) was a disciple who would later travel with Paul. The apostles Paul met were Peter and James, the brother of Jesus (Galatians 1:18-19).

9:29 Here Saul is talking and debating on the Christians' side, just what he would not have done before his conversion.

Galatians

These verses are Paul's own description of what Luke has described in Acts.

1:15 God's hand in Paul's conversion is emphasised here. Without God's intervention no one would be saved.

1:21 Syria and Cilicia - i.e. Paul returned to Tarsus, his home town.

QUESTIONS

1. Look at the following stories of conversion -

    Zacchaeus (Luke 19:1-10)
    the Ethiopian (Acts 8:26-39)
    Paul (Acts 9:3-19)
    Lydia (Acts 16:13-15)
    the jailer (Acts 16:25-34).

    Who initiated each conversion - God or man? What does this teach us about conversion?

2. To convert means to change. Contrast Paul before and after conversion.

VISUAL AID

Map - see page 25. Photocopy at A3 for greater clarity.

FOCUS ACTIVITY

Conversion Bench Ball   Divide the group into 2 teams. One member of each team stands on a chair at opposite ends of the room. The aim is for each team to pass the ball at least 3 times before passing it to the person on the chair for their team to score a goal. If the ball is dropped it is given to the other team to begin passing again. One of the leaders acts as referee to call dropped balls and to shout 'Convert!' every few minutes, at which point the teams change ends with a new catcher on the chair and the game resumes.

At the end of the game comment on what happened whenever 'Convert!' was shouted. Conversion produces a radical change in a person's life. Let's see what happened when Paul was converted to see if this was true of him.

ACTIVITY

Photocopy page 23 for each group member.

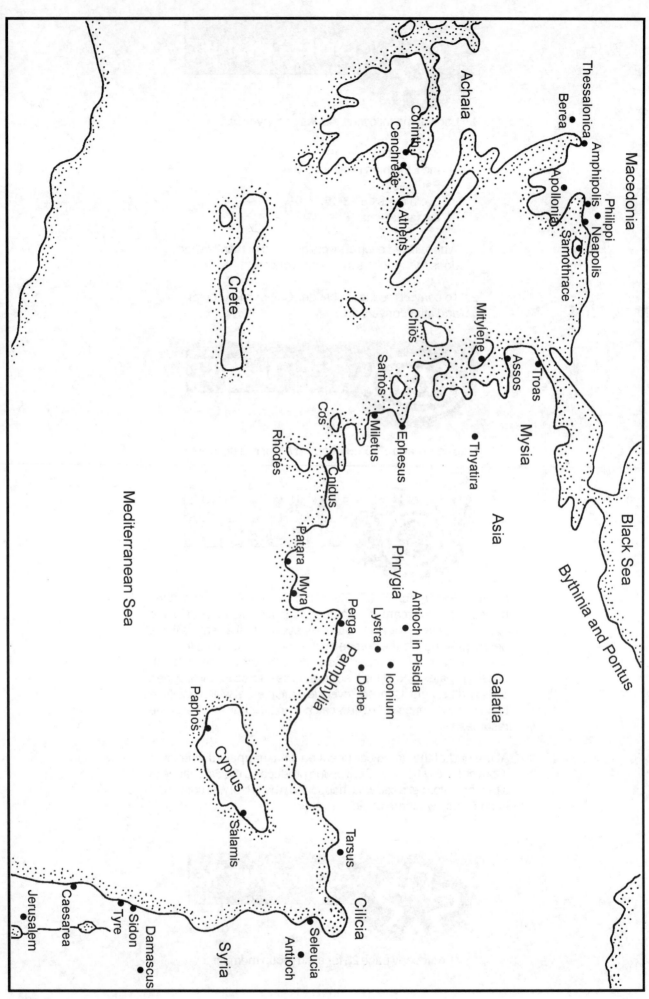

Memory Verse Puzzle

In this puzzle you must discover which letter of the alphabet is represented by each number. The words only read across, and you have been given one word to start you off. If you solve the puzzle you will discover a reassuring statement from the book of Hebrews.

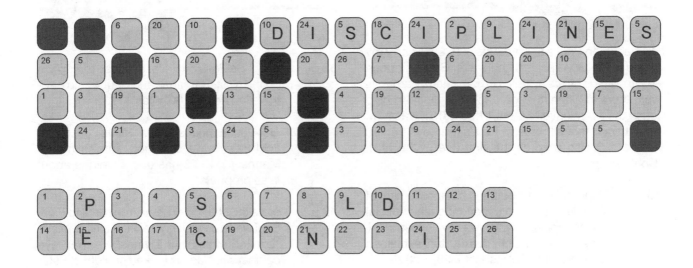

Hebrews 12:10

PREPARATION

Acts 13:1-12

LESSON AIMS

To understand how Paul and Barnabas were commissioned for service.

NB Recap on Paul's calling, Acts 9:15 ... 'to carry my Name to the Gentiles'. 10 years after Saul had been sent to Tarsus by the apostles in Jerusalem, Barnabas went there to ask him to go back to Antioch to help teach the new converts (Acts 11:20-26). It was from this Antioch that all three of Paul's journeys began. Acts 11:26 also records the first use of the term 'Christians'.

13:1   'Church' - not a building but a collection of people. Prophets experienced the special gift of inspiration which was evidenced in OT times. They preached, exhorted, explained and foretold (cf. Acts 11:27-28; 13:32).

        Teachers - cf. 11:26.

13:2   'Worshipping and fasting' - Paul's journeys did not come about after a council decision or committee vote, but rather through the inspiration of the Holy Spirit.

        Some people think that fasting is beneficial in focusing the mind and allowing the person to concentrate on prayer. The mediaeval use of fasting as a means of obtaining grace through denial of the flesh is not what is meant here. Also, do remember that young teens are growing and need regular food intakes!

13:3   More prayer and fasting. These activities need discussion. Points to consider are the setting time aside to pray, both individually and corporately, and the place of fasting.

13:4   Where should they go? Only where the Holy Spirit directed. Seleucia was the nearest sea port to Antioch. Cyprus had already heard the gospel (Acts 11:19-20).

13:5   At least 10 adult males were necessary for the establishment of a synagogue. Paul's policy was always to preach to the Jews first. John, or John Mark, was a cousin of Barnabas, cf. Colossians 4:10.

13:6   From Salamis on the east coast, to Paphos on the west, Barnabas and Saul would have travelled nearly 100 miles.

        Bar-Jesus means son of Jesus. Jesus (or Joshua) was a common Jewish name. Matthew 7:15-23 has dire warnings about false prophets.

13:9   Note the change of name from Saul to Paul. Saul was a Jewish name, Paul a Greek one. 'Looked straight at Elymas', i.e. had eye contact with. Jesus looked straight at Peter when the cock crowed (Luke 22:61).

13:12   He believed when he saw what happened, but only because of the teaching he had received.

QUESTIONS

1. Look up Matthew 6:16-18. Is there a place for fasting in our worship of God? If so, should it always be connected with prayer?

2. What do we learn about sending out missionaries from 13:1-4? Should these same principles be used for every kind of service within the church, e.g. teaching in Sunday School, serving coffee, reading the lesson?

3. It is important to distinguish narrative from teaching sections in the Bible. We need to remember that no Biblical narrative is written expressly about 'us'. God is the hero of all Biblical narratives, so we can learn timeless truths about his dealings with human beings and our response to God's work.

    What can we learn from this passage about God's dealings with man and man's response?

VISUAL AID

Map - see page 22.

FOCUS ACTIVITY

Relays Assign the young people into teams and give each team 2 bowls, one full of water and one empty. Place the full bowl at the start and the empty one at the finish. In between set up obstacles, such as chairs to climb over or run around, tables to wriggle under, etc. Each team has 3 minutes to take it in turns to transport water from the full to the empty bowl using a plastic cup. The winning team is the one to get most water in the bowl at the end of the time period.

Comment on the teams having been given the task of transporting water from place to place. Let's see what task Paul and Barnabas were given and how they set about it.

ACTIVITY

Photocopy page 26 for each group member.

Answer to the puzzle: 1. Simeon
                         2. Cyrene
                         3. Cyprus
                         4. Paphos
                         5. Manaen
                         6. Elymas
                         Rearranged word is Prayer

The name of a person or place from the Bible passage is concealed in each line of letters below. To discover each name take one letter from each group of 3 letters and run them together. The letters you need have been hidden in the correct sequence. Enter your answers in the grid. If you have got it right the shaded letters in the grid can be rearranged to make another word.

1. MSP	IVB	MLO	NLE	DOH	ZCN
2. LCU	DWY	SRX	AEF	KIN	TJE
3. UMC	PYS	GRP	NRA	UCL	OVS
4. PBS	XAF	IWP	HEN	GOL	YES
5. IMY	AOX	AND	FSA	WET	UNC
6. HSE	LBW	GYA	XMC	UKA	SJD

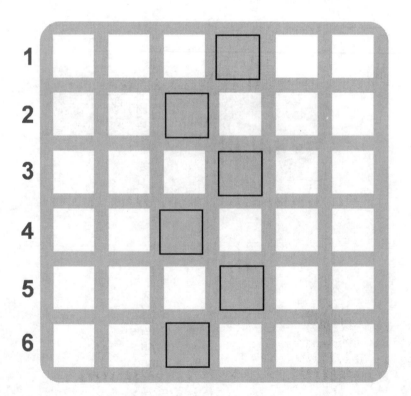

The word is

PREPARATION

Act 13:13-52

LESSON AIMS

To learn the principles of presenting the Gospel.

In this chapter the pattern of Paul's preaching itinerary is established. He goes first to the Jewish synagogue and, if the message is rejected, he then goes out to the Gentiles. Romans 1:16 shows that his reason for doing this was his very real understanding of God's plan of 'salvation for everyone who believes: first for the Jew and then the Gentile.' The synagogue provided a building where preaching was the norm, a congregation who knew their OT Scriptures and a regular preaching pattern on the Sabbath. As most often happened, the Jews were hostile and the Gentiles were the people who heard and believed with joy.

13:13   Perga was the capital of Pamphylia. The reasons for John's departure are not known, but Acts 15:37-39 records Paul's displeasure at John's action.

13:14   Antioch in Pisidia - not Antioch in Syria, where Paul and Barnabas were commissioned.

13:15   As a visiting rabbi, Paul would be asked to speak to the congregation.

13:16   Paul included in his opening remark a reference to the Gentiles, some of whom would be in the congregation.

13:17-22   An outline of God's dealings with his people. Paul began with the knowledge the Jews already had and then built on it.

13:23-31   Paul outlined the story of Jesus, whom he called the Saviour.

13:26   He again made the point of including the Gentiles.

13:27   Paul was clear in his own mind that Jesus' death was foretold in the OT. This would be an amazing thing for the congregation to hear from a rabbi with his credentials.

13:32-41   The challenge of the message. Paul, talking to Jews, used the Scriptures to point to Jesus being the Messiah.

13:39   'Justified from' can mean two different things. Here it means forgiveness of sins, but in Romans 3:21-24 it is the gift of righteousness.

13:42-51   The response.

13:42   Note the interest of the hearers.

13:43   Jews and converts to Judaism were amongst those who showed enthusiasm to hear more.

13:45   The motive here was jealousy. The Jews were jealous of the impact the preaching had on the whole city.

13:48   The Gentiles were glad and honoured God's word.

The doctrine of election will be dealt with in detail in Book 3 week 18.

13:50   The Jews knew who to get on their side. The God-fearing women of high standing and the leading men of the city had the influence to bring about the expulsion of Paul and Barnabas.

13:51-52   Paul and his company are filled with joy and the Holy Spirit despite persecution.

1. Look at Paul's discourse in 13:16-41 and divide it into small sections. Write down what each section is about. What can you learn from this about presenting the gospel?

2. It was Jews and God-fearing women who opposed the gospel. Why? What would they have had to do if they had become believers?

3. What effect does the preaching of the gospel have? (13:42-45,48-50)

Map - see page 22.

Chinese Whispers   Sit the group in a circle. Ask one member to think of a piece of news to pass round the group. The news is whispered from person to person around the group until it gets back to the person who sent it. Continue for 3 or 4 turns, seeing how the news changes each time.

Comment on how efficient that was as a way of broadcasting important information. Let's see what strategy Paul used when passing on the good news about Jesus.

In his discourse to the people at Iconium Paul starts by giving the people a history lesson. Take 8-10 sections from Paul's speech, e.g. the Israelites in Egypt, rescue from Egypt, in the wilderness. Split the class into 2 groups. Mix up the historical order of the sections and give each group 1 section at random. Ask them to choose a specific incident that illustrates that section and mime it to the other group. The groups do this turn and turn about until all the sections have been covered. Then get the class to put the sections into their correct historical order.

PREPARATION

Acts 14:1-28

LESSON AIMS

To understand that preaching the gospel brings opposition.

1. Recap on Acts 9:15-16. Paul was God's chosen instrument to carry his name to the Gentiles and the Jews, and he would suffer for God's sake.

2. Use the map to reinforce the lesson.

14:1-2   Iconium is modern day Konya in Turkey. It was an important route and agricultural centre on the plain of central Galatia.

         'Great numbers of the Jews and Gentiles believed', but then the disbelieving Jews stirred up trouble.

14:3   Paul and Barnabas stayed and continued to preach. The miraculous signs and wonders confirmed the message.

14:4   Division is caused by the preaching of the Gospel.

14:8   Lystra was a Roman colony and the home of Timothy (Acts 16:1). It was about 20 miles from Iconium, where Timothy was also known (16:2).

14:12   Zeus and Hermes were Greek gods and the temple in Lystra was dedicated to Zeus, the king of the gods. Hermes was a messenger, so Paul was given this title, whilst Barnabas was called Zeus, because probably he was the more imposing of the 2 men.

14:19   Paul's suffering is really beginning, as God had promised.

14:21-25   Paul and Barnabas make a return trip to all the new churches - Lystra, Iconium, and Antioch, where opposition to the Gospel had sprung up.

14:22   'Strengthening ... encouraging ... remain true to the faith'. Paul didn't leave converts to fend for themselves. His purpose was that

they should be built up as strong Christians. 'Endure hardships' cf. Luke 9:23.

14:23   The pattern of elders for the early church is established, underpinned by prayer and fasting (cf. 13:3).

14:27   Mission completed! They report to the church, who commissioned them, and they emphasise the effect of the Gospel on the Gentiles.

14:28   A long time was probably a year.

QUESTIONS

1. Summarise the places visited on the first missionary journey. What pattern of preaching and what results are beginning to emerge?

2. What experiences has Paul suffered on this journey for the sake of the Gospel (cf. 2 Corinthians 11:23-31)? What is his attitude to suffering?

VISUAL AID

Map - see page 22.

Run the Distance   Designate one person to be 'It' and a distance for the rest of the group to run, e.g. from one wall to another. 'It' can only run across the course. The group members have to run from start to finish without being tagged. Anyone who is tagged also becomes 'It', so a wall of people is gradually built up, which needs to be run through to get to the finishing point.

Point out how difficult it became to get to the finishing point as opposition built up. Let's see what Paul did when he encountered opposition.

ACTIVITY

Photocopy page 31 for each group member.

During his journeys Paul learnt an important lesson. Answer the following questions to discover what it was. The answers have been broken into groups of letters which can be found in the grid. As you answer each question cross off the relevant letters.

GUE	HAR	ES	DN	ODN	SYN
SAC	OND	ICO	CH	FAI	ERS
UM	KIN	GO	FIC	SIG	TIO
IPS	AGO	AN	EWS	RI	ELD
ERS	TH	ESS	NSW	DSH	NI

1. In which town were Paul and Barnabas at the beginning of this chapter? (7)

2. Where did Paul and Barnabas go on first entering a town? (9)

3. What did God give Paul and Barnabas power to do as a confirmation of their message? (5 and 7)

4. What did Paul and Barnabas continue to preach at Lystra and Derbe? (4,4)

5. What did the crippled man have to be healed? (5)

6. What did the crowd at Lystra want to offer to Paul and Barnabas? (10)

7. What did God show mankind by sending rain from heaven and crops in their season? (8)

8. Who did Paul and Barnabas appoint in each church? (6)

9. To which town did Paul and Barnabas return at the end of their journey? (7)

Now write the remaining groups of letters in the right order to complete the verse.

We must go through many .... to enter the kingdom of God.

Which verse is this from?   Acts 14:

31

PREPARATION

Acts 15:1-35

LESSON AIMS

To distinguish between God's laws made for all time and those that were given for a particular period.

In these verses the clash between the Jewish traditionalists, who had been converted, and the Gentile believer begins to emerge. For the Jewish party (Judaisers) it was abhorrent that believers were not circumcised as the Mosaic Law required. Circumcision was a sign of belonging to God's people (Genesis 17:10-14). In addition, to eat meat with blood still in it was another violation of the God-given rules. Leviticus 17:10-14 states clearly that blood must be drained off meat before consumption. The blood signified the life of the animal and blood shed was an atonement for sins.

15:1   Antioch is north of Jerusalem, which is the capital of Judea. Some men who held that circumcision was a mark of the believer came from the church at Jerusalem and tried to influence the believers. Acts 15:24 shows that they were not authorised by the apostles.

15:2   The centre of the church was still in Jerusalem.

15:4-5   There was a meeting of the whole church to welcome the Antioch party, and the clash came out into the open.

15:6-11   The apostles and elders withdrew to make a policy decision.

15:7   Peter argued from his own experience with Cornelius (Acts 10:28-29).

15:8   God's seal of salvation is the Holy Spirit (Acts 10:44,47).

15:12-22   This section takes place before the whole church. The decision of the elders and the apostles is passed on to the whole congregation.

15:12   Barnabas is listed before Paul, perhaps because he was more important in Jerusalem. Barnabas had introduced Paul

to the apostles after his conversion (Acts 9:26-27).

15:16-18   Amos 9:11-12.

15:19-21   Circumcision is not required but 4 other instructions are given to the Gentiles to avoid further difficulties. They had to avoid -
1. 'Food polluted by idols' i.e. sacrificed to them.
2. Sexual immorality - in Greek society sexual practices were lax.
3. Strangled animals i.e. those containing the blood, not having been hung properly.
4. Blood - maybe having the blood apart from the meat.

All these conditions affected either the believer's relationship with God or his relationship with other Christians -

food offered to idols was to do with the worship of other gods,

sexual immorality desecrated God's 'temple' (the body),

meat with blood in it prevented fellowship with devout Jewish Christians.

15:21   James reminded his hearers that there was no danger of the Mosaic Law being forgotten as it was read every Sabbath in the synagogue.

15:22   Action was agreed by the whole church. Silas is to be a partner in Paul's next missionary journey.

15:23-30   The letter and the return to Antioch. The pattern of apostolic authority is beginning to emerge. The theological decision has been taken by the apostles and agreed to by the whole church.

15:32   The prophet's function here was to encourage and build up the early church.

QUESTIONS

1. The men from Jerusalem said that to be a **real** Christian you had to be circumcised as well as believe the gospel. Do **we** add special conditions to the gospel, e.g. confirmation, adult baptism, special signs of the Holy Spirit's presence, etc?

2. In Galatians 3:23-25 Paul says that the believer is no longer under the supervision of the law. How does this tie in with the edict of the Jerusalem church (v.28-29)? How do we decide what parts of the OT law we should keep? (Look up 1 Corinthians 10:23-33 for help.)

FOCUS ACTIVITY

Can you spot a fake? Show the group various items, some of which are real and some fake, e.g. does a piece of jewellery contain real gems or paste? Also ask leaders to make claims about themselves, some of which are true and some false. Ask the group to vote on whether the item or statement is real/true or fake/false.

Comment on how difficult it can be to spot the fake. In Paul's day the church had to find a way of deciding who were the real believers in Jesus. Let's see what they came up with.

ACTIVITY

Photocopy page 34 for each group member.

At the Council of Jerusalem Paul and Barnabas reported to the apostles and elders how God had saved the Gentiles. Enter every word of the Bible verse below into the crossword grid. Underline each word as you position it. When you have finished the letters in the shaded squares will spell something we must not do to the Gospel.

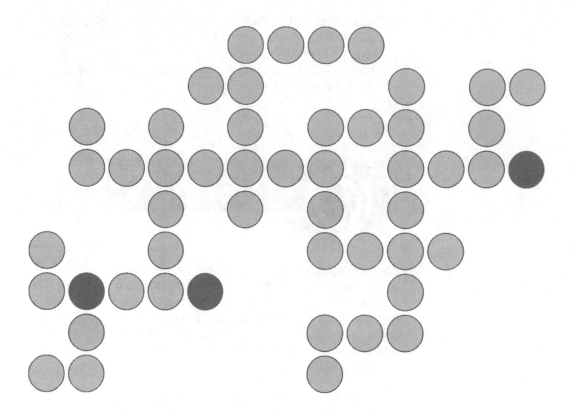

We believe it is through the grace of our Lord Jesus that we are saved, just as they are.

Acts 15:11

We must not .... to the Gospel.

PREPARATION

Acts 15:36 - 16:15

LESSON AIMS

To learn what qualities should be demonstrated in the life of the Christian.

This passage splits into 4 sections (15:36-41; 16:1-5; 16:6-10; 16:11-15). In this study we will concentrate on the qualities that should be demonstrated by a Christian who is trying to share his faith (this includes all of us!). In the first section Paul refuses to take John Mark with him because of his unreliability. By contrast, the second section deals with Timothy, who is spoken well of by the Christians in his locality. These verses also deal with Timothy being circumcised so as not to cause needless offence. This is a useful lesson for young teens, who are often ungracious in the way they speak to their peers who disagree with them. In the third section we see Paul's sensitivity to the leading of the Holy Spirit and the final verses show Lydia generously demonstrating hospitality.

15:36   Paul is anxious to leave Antioch to visit the new churches he had started.

15:39   Barnabas and his cousin Mark, or John Mark, do not appear again in Acts after the dispute with Paul. Even though they part company there is a reference in 1 Corinthians 9:6 to Barnabas being a worker like Paul. After his work with Barnabas, Mark eventually joined Peter and heard of the things said and done by Jesus, later recorded in his Gospel. At a later date Paul is reunited with Mark (Colossians 4:10), and in 2 Timothy 4:11 Paul requests Mark to join him in his final days of imprisonment.

15:40   Silas had returned to Jerusalem after delivering the apostolic letter (15:33). He must have returned to Antioch, presumably to do church work.

16:1   Timothy, probably still in his teens, may have been a convert at Paul's earlier visit. His mother's faith is mentioned, and the silence about his Greek father would suggest no interest in Judaism or Christianity.

16:3   This would seem a contradiction of the apostolic order from the Jerusalem Council. In spite of having a Greek father, Timothy had been brought up as a Jew (2 Timothy

3:14-15) so Paul was regularising the situation so that needless offence would not be caused. It had nothing to do with circumcision being a prerequisite of salvation.

16:4-5   Obedience to the apostolic commands strengthened the faith of the church.

16:6   Paul's companions were Silas and Timothy.

16:6-7   The Spirit of Jesus (or the Holy Spirit) was their guide.

16:8   Troas was 10 miles from the ancient city of Troy. It was a Roman colony and a busy seaport. A church was started here either on this journey or the next.

16:11   'We' - Luke, the author of Acts, has now joined them.

16:12   Philippi was a Roman colony and an important city in the area. It was named after Alexander the Great's father, Philip II. As there were only a few Jews there was no synagogue. Paul later wrote a letter to the church at Philippi, which will be studied in the next series.

16:13   If there was no synagogue it was customary for the Jews to meet outdoors near running water.

16:14   Lydia is a Greek name. She was from Thyatira, which was known for its purple dye (royal colour). See Revelation 1:11 where it is one of the 7 churches to receive a letter from the risen Christ. Like Cornelius, Lydia was a devout Gentile who believed in the true God and followed the moral teachings of the OT. Immediately she heard the message of salvation she responded (cf. Luke 24:45).

16:15   Baptism and hospitality follow after her conversion (cf. Romans 12:13).

QUESTIONS

1. Luke is faithful in recording the events of this period. He does not gloss over the difficulty between Paul and Barnabas. Do Christians always agree? How should differences be handled? (See Philippians 2:1-7 for help).

2. Look at the 4 sections of the passage (15:36-41; 16:1-5; 16:6-10; 16:11-15). What can you learn from John Mark, Timothy, Paul and Lydia about the qualities required by a Christian seeking to share his/her faith?

VISUAL AID

Map - see page 22.

FOCUS ACTIVITY

Guess the Occupation Describe 4 different training schedules or lifestyles to the group and ask them to guess the occupation of the person. E.g. 'I get up, eat a healthy breakfast, stretch out my muscles, put on my trainers and grab my stopwatch. What is my profession?' Answer: athlete. You could use pictures, types of clothing, magazines, etc. as props. One or two members of the group could also think of an occupation and describe it.

Suggested occupations: chef, singer, artist, doctor or nurse.
Point out that people behave in a way that is appropriate to their occupation. In the same way, being a Christian affects the whole of life. Let's see how that was true of the people in today's Bible study.

ACTIVITY

Photocopy page 37 for each group member. The Bible verse is the memory verse for the Paul series in weeks 16-18.

Memory Verse Puzzle

Paul travelled to many different places, mostly on foot. To discover one of his instructions to the church at Philippi, start at the little toe and trace the Bible verse through the maze. You can only move along straight lines. Use every letter, but no letter is used more than once. As you go add arrows to the lines so that you can retrace your journey if necessary. Write the verse at the foot of the page.

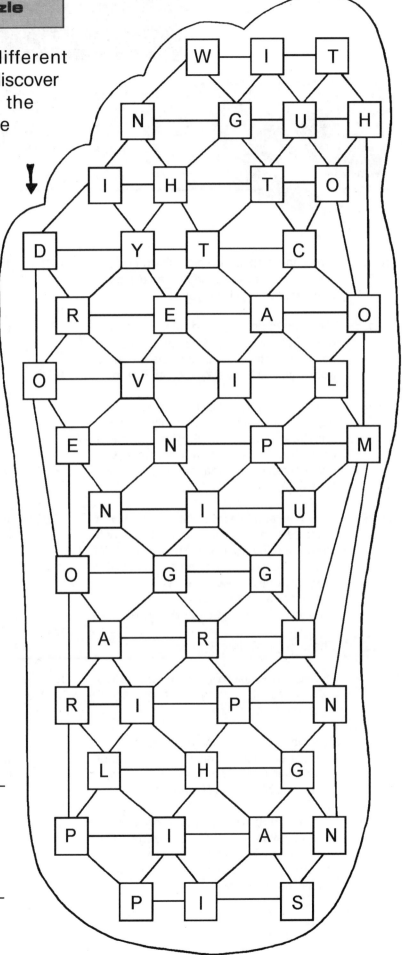

Verse

– – – – – – – – – – – – –

– – – – – –

– – – – – – – – – – – –

– – – – – – – – – – .

2:14

PREPARATION

Acts 16:16-40

LESSON AIMS

To learn how a Christian should react when punished unjustly.

16:16 'Who had a spirit by which she predicted the future' - the slave girl had an evil spirit with the power of clairvoyance.

16:17 'The rest of us' - the next reference to the writer, Luke, is in 20:5 where the story again continues in the first person. It is assumed from that, that Luke stayed on in Philippi.

16:18 After several days, Paul proceeded to cast out the evil spirit by the authority of Jesus. The slave girl had been telling the truth about Paul and Silas, but this witness was unacceptable from that source (see also Luke 8:28).

16:19 Only Paul and Silas were arrested, maybe because they were the only fully Jewish members of the group, or the more important. Note the reason for their arrest - 'their (the owners) hope of making money was gone'. The market square in Philippi was a business centre which has now been excavated.

16:20-21 The charge falls into 2 parts -

a) Causing a public disturbance, backed by anti-Jewish feeling (which was not unknown at the time).

b) Advocating non-Roman customs - foreign cults (including Christianity) were not tolerated under Roman law; Judaism was acceptable and had legal status.

16:22 'Stripped and beaten' - this was allowed under Roman law for non-Roman citizens. The authorities carried bundles of rods with which to carry out their duties, and as a sign of magisterial authority.

16:24 Inner cells and stocks were for extra security.

16:27 cf. Acts 12:19. A guard's life was taken if a prisoner escaped, so the jailer was saving himself the degradation of a public execution.

16:30 The jailer had heard what these men had been teaching. Confronted with a threat of death, and with the experience of an earthquake, he needed to find out about salvation.

16:32 The word of the Lord tells the way of salvation (Romans 10:17).

16:33-34 His conversion results in his immediate care for the prisoners, and his request for baptism. This is another instance of a whole household being baptised on hearing the word of the Lord and believing (see also 16:15).

16:34 Joy because of belief in God, not because of outward circumstances.

16:37 If Paul and Silas had left jail without challenging the authorities, it could have left the early church in Philippi very vulnerable to arbitrary treatment. Roman citizens were expressly exempt from beating, so Paul wanted a public apology in order to protect the church.

16:39 The request to leave the city was to forestall further trouble from the slave girl's owners and the crowd.

16:40 'They left' - i.e. Luke stayed on.

QUESTIONS

1. What can we learn from the motive of the slave girl's owners for getting rid of Paul and Silas (1 Timothy 6:10)?

2. What can we learn from Paul's attitude in prison to help us when we suffer as a Christian? When should we stand up for our rights and when should we 'turn the other cheek' (Matthew 5:38-42)?

FOCUS ACTIVITY

Hang in there!   Ask for a couple of volunteers who think that they have good balance. Ask them to stand on one leg, then ask the rest of the group to do things to try and throw them off balance. Suggestions are putting on a blindfold, balancing a book on their head, asking them to hold a heavy object, asking them to say something repeatedly or sing, etc. The winner is the one who lasts longest without putting the other foot down or falling over.

Will you hang in there when the going gets tough? Let's see whether Paul did.

ACTIVITY

This is a good one for the group to act. Split the class in half and ask each group to prepare a play from the passage to act to each other. They may want to do a modern adaptation using a situation where Christians are persecuted for their faith. Each group is responsible for organising themselves. They should appoint a director, who can then decide with his/her group on the script, allocate parts, etc.

OVERVIEW
Philippians

Week 11 | **Prayer** | *Philippians 1:1-11*
To understand more about prayer.

Week 12 | **Rejoicing** | *Philippians 1:12-30*
To teach that the chief end of man is to glorify God and to enjoy him forever.

Week 13 | **Humility** | *Philippians 2:1-30*
To understand the meaning of true humility.

Week 14 | **The Race** | *Philippians 3:1 - 4:1*
To show the importance of perseverance in the Christian's life.

Week 15 | **Peace and Contentment** | *Philippians 4:2-23*
To learn more of the all-sufficiency of Christ

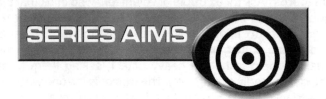

SERIES AIMS

1. To develop a deeper understanding of the person and work of the Lord Jesus.

2. To understand that, although the Christian life will be hard, the Christian has ultimately security and hope in the life eternal.

MEMORY WORK

Your attitude should be the same as that of Christ Jesus:
Who, being in very nature God,
did not consider equality with God something to be grasped,
but made himself nothing,
taking the very nature of a servant,
being made in human likeness.

And being found in appearance as a man,
he humbled himself
and became obedient to death - even death on a cross!

Therefore God exalted him to the highest place
and gave him the name that is above every name,
that at the name of Jesus every knee should bow,
in heaven and on earth and under the earth,
and every tongue confess that Jesus Christ is Lord,
to the glory of God the Father.

Philippians 2:5-11

Philippians

The Philippian church was founded by Paul, Silas and Timothy in approximately AD 50-52 during Paul's second missionary journey. Luke was also present, as is shown by his use of the pronoun 'we' (Acts 16:16). After Paul left Philippi it is likely that Luke stayed on, helping to build up the new church. Timothy or Silas possibly visited the church later as well. Paul next came to Philippi on his 3rd missionary journey (Acts 20:6).

Philippi was a prosperous Roman colony (Acts 16:12) and was situated on the Egnatian Way, the road from Asia Minor to Rome. It was named after Philip of Macedon, who founded it in 360 BC. A gold mining industry was developed and coins were minted. In 168 BC Macedonia was annexed by the Romans and split into 4 districts. Philippi was the leading city in the 1st district. Following Octavius' battles with Brutus and Cassius in 42 BC and with Anthony and Cleopatra in 31 BC Philippi was colonised by Italian settlers. It was then given the status of a Roman colony with the same rights and privileges that were enjoyed by the citizens of Rome. Women had a high status in Macedonia and took an active part in public and business life. The Acts account tells us that there was no synagogue in Philippi and the early believers were largely Gentile, e.g. the jailer and Lydia. For this reason the letter to them has no OT references.

The letter to the Philippians makes clear that Paul was writing from prison. Most scholars think that this was his first Roman imprisonment, which means the letter was written between AD 61-63. At that time he was under house arrest and supervised by the Praetorian guard, a crack division of Imperial troops who had special privileges and pay (Acts 28:16-20). Part of their duties was to mount guard over the prisoners who were awaiting trial before Caesar. Paul's witness to these men had an effect on the whole palace guard (Philippians 1:13). They also heard the conversations Paul had with his visitors (Acts 28:30-31). At the time of writing Timothy was with Paul.

Following his release Paul may have visited Philippi a 3rd time, on his 4th missionary journey. He was eventually re-arrested and executed at the hand of the Emperor Nero around AD 67.

From the letter we know a bit about the Philippian church. It was big enough to need overseers (bishops) and deacons (administrators) (Philippians 1:1). It was a suffering church (1:29) and a generous church (4:15-18), but was troubled with disunity (2:2-4,14; 4:2). There may also have been a perfectionist group within the church (3:12-13) as well as a group pushing the need for circumcision (3:2-3). The letter was written to deal with these points as well as to thank the Philippians for the gift they had sent to him with Epaphroditus. It also commended Timothy and Epaphroditus to them and explained why Epaphroditus was returning to Philippi.

Joy is a key theme of the book. Paul possibly had a death sentence hanging over him, but despite this he was able to rejoice. Throughout the book we see Paul's concern for the church he had planted and the centrality of the Lord Jesus in his life and work.

PREPARATION

Philippians 1:1-11

LESSON AIMS

To understand more about prayer.

It is important to set the scene by having a brief look at life in Philippi and the founding of the church (see Series Overview and Acts 16:12-40).
This passage can be divided into two parts:

a) 1:1-2   the greeting
b) 1:3-11   the thanksgiving and prayer of Paul.

1:1   Paul follows the conventional format of a letter of his time:

        a) the name of the sender(s)
        b) the name(s) of the recipients
        c) the greeting.

        Timothy was not the co-author but was with Paul in Rome when this letter was written (2:19) and was known to the Philippian Christians (Acts 16).

        Servants - in the service of Christ Jesus. The word used implies the recognition of Christ's authority and a total submission to his will. This would have been shocking language for the Greek hearers. Isaiah 42:1 describes Jesus as the 'servant' of the Lord. 'Saints' is a name applicable to all Christians and means 'set apart'. It comes from the Greek 'hagios'.

        Note the use of 'all'. Right at the beginning Paul includes everyone. This is important in view of the disunity present in the church.

1:3-4   'Thank God', 'in all my prayers', 'I always pray for you with joy'. Paul's prayers are characterised by their frequency, fervour and thankfulness to God.

1:5   'Your partnership in the gospel' - not merely their conversion but their active support of his ministry (cf. 4:15). Paul is at great pains to promote team spirit. Note also the repetition of the word 'all' (v.4,7,8).

1:6   'Confident', 'good work will be completed'. God's work in salvation of souls will be completed on the day of Jesus' return. It is only then that perfection will be achieved.

1:7   'Share in God's grace with me' - the Philippians had sent Epaphroditus with gifts for Paul whilst in prison. They had been one with him in his persecution.

1:8   Paul's concern, compassion and love for them is based on his union with Christ Jesus.

1:9   'Love may abound ..... in knowledge and depth of insight'. Real love requires growth based on knowledge and understanding.

1:10   'Discern what is best', 'pure and blameless' - the ongoing process of sanctification. The Philippians need knowledge (v.9) to enable them to differentiate between real and bogus spirituality.

1:11   Fruits of righteousness - cf. Galatians 5:22. Fruit is expected in the life of a Christian through abiding in Jesus the vine (John 15:5).

QUESTIONS

1. Look up each time Paul uses 'all' in these verses. What does this teach about the standing of the ordinary Christian?

2. What things does Paul pray for the Philippians? How do these compare with the way we pray for others?

3. Why does Paul mention the day of Christ twice in these verses (v.6,10)?

Brainstorming   Using a whiteboard, flip chart or large sheet of paper, write the word 'prayer' in a thought bubble in the centre. Ask the group to brainstorm the topic and write down any relevant thoughts.

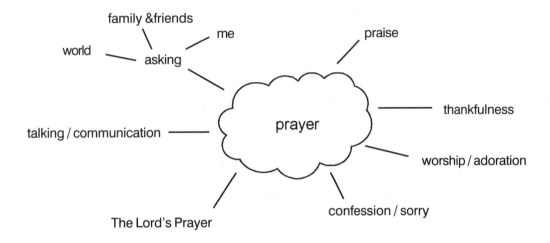

Let's see what we can learn from one of Paul's prayers.

ACTIVITY

Photocopy page 44 for each group member.

Using your Bible, answer the following questions and insert your answers in the grid. When you have finished, the letters in the shaded column will spell the missing word from the Bible verse below.

1. Paul's greeting (v.2).

2. What love needs (v.9).

3. Paul's friend in Rome (v.1).

4. What we need to be (v.10).

5. What we need to show (v.9).

6. How Paul describes himself (v.1).

7. What must grow in a Christian's life (v.11).

8. What Paul feels about God's work in their lives (v.6).

9. What Paul and the Philippians were partners in (v.5).

10. What we need to do (v.10).

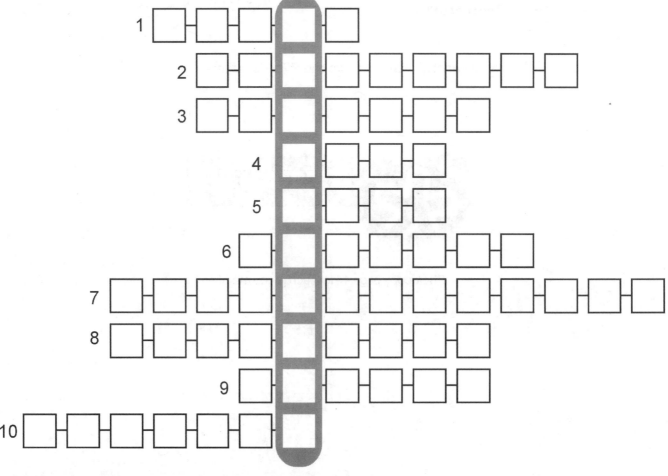

He who began a good work in you will carry it on to ....
Which verse is this from?

PREPARATION

Philippians 1:12-30

LESSON AIMS

To teach that the chief end of man is to glorify God and to enjoy him forever.

After the greetings, thanksgiving and prayer of the previous verses, Paul gives the Philippian church news about himself. These verses give us a glimpse of Paul's life inside prison. The letter would have been read aloud to the Philippians, who would no doubt be anxious to find out what was happening to Paul. Verses 12-26 contain Paul's testimony and therefore the verses are full of 'I' and 'me'. Paul looks back to the past (v.12), in verses 13-18 he writes about the present, and in 19-26 he probes the future. The last verses, 27-30, are an encouragement to the Philippian church to continue in their faith. The over-riding theme which shines through this passage is the centrality of the Lord Jesus in Paul's life. The glory of Christ was his controlling interest and must be ours.

The Past

1:12   'What has happened to me' - this includes all the events from his conversion on the way to Damascus to his imprisonment in Rome, such as lynching, flogging, insult, misrepresentation, storm at sea, and two years under house arrest.

'Really' - despite the list of burdens, Paul sees God's over-ruling hand in his circumstances. Suffering is not a sign of God's displeasure but is to be expected; we are not greater than our master (2:8, 2 Timothy 3:12).

The Present

1:13   Paul was under house arrest (see series overview regarding the Praetorian guard). No doubt the guards heard Paul's testimony and witnessed sessions between Paul and those who visited him (Acts 28:30).

1:14   A second effect of his imprisonment was to stir up the Christians in Rome to bolder and more effective witness.

1:15-17   'Some preach Christ out of envy and rivalry ... out of selfish ambition, not sincerely, supposing that they can stir up trouble for

me'. We can assume that these people were not Judaisers or people from the circumcision party or Paul would have characteristically condemned their message, e.g. Galatians 1:6-9. However, he is reticent about them, giving little detail. 1 Corinthians 13:5 could show his motive, 'Love is not resentful, it keeps no record of wrong'. It has been suggested that they were Christians who were jealous of Paul, his gifts and his apostolic fame. When he came to Rome they resented his presence and the threat (as they perceived it) to their status.

1:18   Confirms that these people were Christians, as they did preach the gospel.

'Rejoice' - a word frequently used in this letter. Paul was in chains and under attack from fellow Christians yet he was able to rejoice.

The Future

1:19   'The Spirit of Jesus Christ' - the Holy Spirit is not only the Spirit of God the Father (Romans 8:9) but also the Spirit of Christ (Acts 16:7).

Deliverance could here be from prison, or the final deliverance from this life into the next. verse 25 would suggest Paul meant the former.

1:20   Courage is what Paul needed to keep going.

1:21-22   Here is the secret of Paul's life. His whole being and purpose for living was in Christ himself.

'Fruitful labour' - the spread of the gospel.

1:23   After death the believer is with Christ. Paul is certain of his final destination but unsure of how and when he will get there.

Encouragement to the Philippians

1:27   When the gospel is threatened Christians must stand together.

'The faith of the gospel' - an apostolic church is one based on apostolic teaching.

1:28   'A sign' - opposition to the church and the gospel is a sign of eventual destruction, since it involves a rejection of the only way of salvation. Similarly, if Christians are persecuted for their faith it is a sign that their salvation is genuine (2 Thessalonians 1:5).

1:29   'Granted to suffer' - cf. 1 Peter 4:14. It is a gift or a privilege to suffer for the gospel. This is not a popular idea!

1:30   'Same struggle you saw I had'. Whilst in Philippi Paul and Silas had been imprisoned, stripped and flogged. The Philippians could also expect to find hardship in their Christian life.

1. How had suffering helped advance the gospel (v.12-14)?

2. How might you be called to suffer as a Christian? Can you give an example?

3. What gives Paul reason to rejoice (v.18-19)?

4. Why is the unity of Christians important (v.27-30)?

The Adverb Game   Ask for a volunteer to act something to the rest of the group. Give the volunteer a slip of paper containing a task plus adverb, e.g. recite a nursery rhyme quietly. The group have to guess the adverb. The one who guesses correctly is the next one to act. Continue for several turns, finishing with doing something joyfully or rejoicingly.

Suggested tasks: walk round the room, dance a jig, mime getting up in the morning, write a letter, etc.

Suggested adverbs: clumsily, sadly, gently, lovingly, impatiently, etc.

Discuss what it means to rejoice and when we do it. Let's see what Paul has to say about when we should rejoice.

Photocopy page 47 for each group member.

Find the following words in the word square. Each word reads backwards or forwards in a straight line horizontally, vertically or diagonally. No letter is used more than once.

AMBITION
ASHAMED
BROTHERS
CHAINS
CHOOSE
CHRIST
COURAGEOUSLY

DEATH
DELIVERANCE
DEPART
DESTROYED
ENVY
FAITH
FEARLESSLY
FRUITFUL

GOODWILL
JOY
LABOUR
LIFE
LORD
PALACE GUARD
PRAYERS
PREACH

REJOICE
REMAIN
RIVALRY
SAVED
SELFISH
WAY
WORTHY

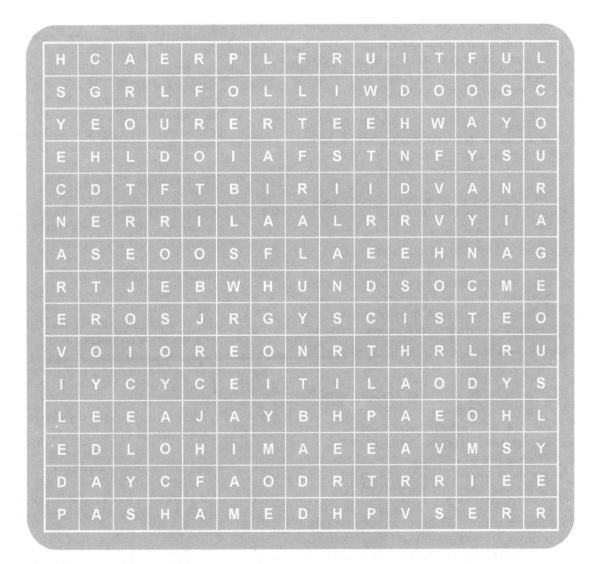

Now, starting from the top and reading from left to right, write down the remaining letters in the blanks below to discover why we are here.
The chief end of man is to _ _ _ _ _ _ _ God and _ _ _ _ _ _ _ _
_ _ _ _ _ _ _ _ _ _ _ . *(Westminster Shorter Catechism)*

PREPARATION

Philippians 2:1-30

LESSON AIMS

To understand the meaning of true humility.

These verses can be divided into 3 sections:
1. v.1-4,12-18   Instructions to the Philippians
2. v.5-11   The person and position of the Lord Jesus Christ.
3. v.19-30   Epaphroditus and Timothy.

2:2-3   See series overview. One of Paul's reasons for writing was to encourage unity in the church. In chapter 4:2 this is developed further. Unity does not mean uniformity but a common aim when working together.

2:3   'Selfish ambition or vain conceit' - these 2 attitudes would harm the fellowship, cf. 1:17.

2:5   'Attitude' or mind set.

2:6-11   These verses are possibly an early Christian hymn.

2:6   'Very nature God'. Jesus was fully God.

'Something to be grasped' could mean something to be forcibly retained. Jesus was willing to give up the glory of heaven (cf. John 17:5) and suffer the humiliation of being a man, but he did not give up any of his essential deity.

2:7   'Made himself nothing' or 'emptied himself' - as Wesley puts it:
'Emptied himself of all but love
And bled for Adam's helpless race.'
'Nature of a servant' - as a servant he would submit to the will of his master, in this case to God the Father (cf. Matthew 20:28).

2:10-11   'Every knee shall bow ... every tongue confess' - ultimately all will have to acknowledge the Lordship of Christ, though not every one will be saved.

2:12   Because of the unique example of Christ's obedience and humility, the commands from God through Paul to the Philippians are to be obeyed.

'My presence' - i.e. during his 2nd and 3rd missionary journeys (Acts 16 and 20).

'Work out your salvation' does not mean a gospel of works but a lifetime process of growth in which the believer has to be actively involved.

'Fear and trembling' - in reverence for God's grace.

2:14   No complaining at God's will. Paul was in a position where he could tell them not to complain. He had every reason, humanly speaking, to complain about his circumstances.

2:15   'Shine as stars' cf. Daniel 12:3.

2:17   'Being poured out' may refer to his whole life's work, or to his present condition which could lead to a martyr's death.

2:19-24   Timothy's association with Paul.

2:19   Paul is planning to send Timothy to visit the church in Philippi so that he can report back to Paul on their progress.

2:20   Timothy's attitude is like the one Paul envisaged in 2:4.

2:22   Timothy served with Paul. He displayed the servant attitude of 1:1.

2:24   Paul here is hopeful of release.

2:25   Epaphroditus is called brother, fellow-worker, fellow-soldier. Paul's commendation is very high.

2:25   A messenger - see series overview.

2:28   Paul's intention is for Epaphroditus to return to Philippi to stay, whereas Timothy would return to Paul in Rome.

1. What is true humility (v.3)? Why is it not a virtue commended by the people in the world?

2. Do we have 'rights', e.g. women's rights, children's rights?

3. What does it mean 'to work out your own salvation' (v.12-13)? What examples are given in 1:27 - 2:16?

FOCUS ACTIVITY

Articulate   This can be played in one or more groups, depending on the number of young people. Each group is given a pile of cards with one word written on each. The cards are placed face down on the table. One member of the group takes a card and describes the word without using the word on the card. The rest of the group try to guess the word being described. The person who guesses correctly picks up the next card. Continue until all the cards have been used, seeing how well the words are described. If playing this as a team game, the first team to complete the task wins.

Suggested words: obedient, unity, complaining, selfish, servant, humility. Finish with humility.

Let's see what Paul has to say about the true meaning of humility.

ACTIVITY

Photocopy page 50 for each group member.

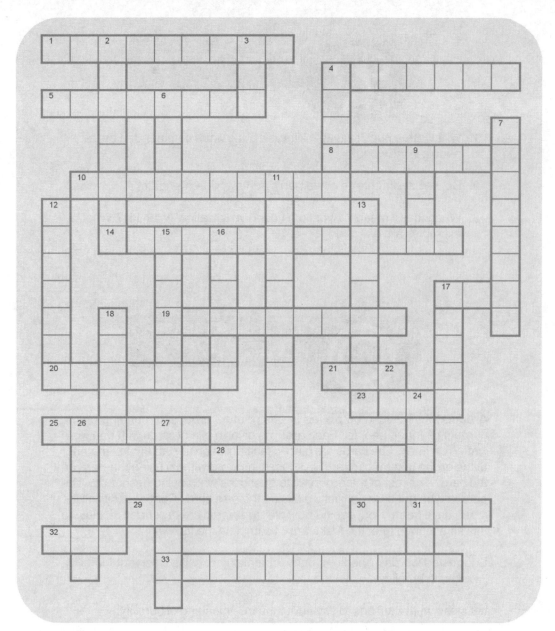

Across

1. What Paul was poured out on (v.17)
4. What comes from Christ's love (v.1)
5. Our attitude as we consider others (v.3)
8. What nature Jesus took (v.7)
10. One of the qualities in verse 1
14. The result of being united with Christ (v.1)
17. The opposite of happy
19. What people look out for (v.21)
20. What God has done for Jesus (v.9)
21. What every knee will do (v.10)
23. What Timothy will bring Paul (v.19)
25. Whose interests we should be concerned with (v.4)
28. What Jesus did not grasp (v.6)
29. The one who works in us (v.13)
30. In what likeness was Jesus made? (v.7)
32. Paul did not do this for nothing (v.16)
33. What we must not do (v.14)

Down

2. What Paul's joy was to be made (v.2)
3. What the Psalmist asks God to hear (Psalm 142:6)
4. Where Jesus died (v.8)
6. What Jesus is (v.11)
7. What should be the same as Jesus? (v.5)
9. The type of conceit (v.3)
11. The name of the Philippians' messenger (v.25)
12. The kind of interest Timothy took (v.20)
13. What is selfish? (v.3)
15. The Greek word for Messiah
16. The relationship with Jesus (v.1)
17. What we shine like (v.15)
18. The result of obedience for Jesus (v.8)
22. Another word for us
24. The first name for Christians (Acts 9:2)
26. What will confess Jesus as Lord? (v.11)
27. Paul's command (v.18)
31. What Jesus became (v.8)

PREPARATION

Philippians 3:1 - 4:1

LESSON AIMS

To show the importance of perseverance in the Christian life.

3:1   'Finally' - it seems that Paul was beginning to dictate a conclusion, but there is an abrupt change between verses 1 and 2. A possible explanation for this break is that Paul was interrupted with news of the renewed activities of Judaisers.

3:2   'Dogs', 'mutilators of the flesh' - these terms show Paul's strength of feeling about the teaching of these men, who would seem to be bringing Christians under the Mosaic law (cf. Galatians 5:15) as a prerequisite for salvation.

3:3   'We who are the circumcision' - the true circumcision is realised by those who have become Christians, who worship by the Spirit, who glory in Jesus Christ, who have no confidence in the flesh.

3:4-7   Paul's list of qualifications would be commendable to the Jews; all are inherited, except his choice of becoming a Pharisee.

3:7   But all the list of advantages Paul now regards as loss or rubbish (v.8).

3:9   'Be found in him' - refers to a continuing experience of a relationship with Christ, the righteousness that comes from God (cf. Romans 3:21-22).

3:10   'Know Christ' - not just an academic knowledge, but an experience of Christ's resurrection power. Fellowship with the risen Christ meant sharing in his sufferings.

3:11   'Somehow' - this is not an indication of doubt, but expresses certainty in spite of not knowing **how** it will all happen (see 1:20-21).

3:12-16   The Runner. The Christian life is likened here and in other scriptures to an athletic race (cf. Hebrews 12:1).

3:12   'Take hold of that ... took hold of me' - God 'took hold' of Paul on the road to Damascus, and Paul's goal is what Christ wants for him.

3:13   'Forgetting' - leaving behind his past, not being hampered by it (see v.4-6).

3:14   In a Greek race the winner received a wreath of flowers and sometimes a cash reward. Christians receive everlasting glory.

3:16   We are responsible for living lives reflecting the truth of what we know.

3:19   'Their destiny is destruction', 'stomach', 'shame', 'earthly things'. Paul here is talking about people who have set their minds on earthly things - the earthly desires of the flesh come first. They are probably libertines or Antinomians rather than the legalists of v.2. (Antinomians believe that Christians are not bound by the moral law so need not keep it.) However it could be that Paul was referring to the fact that the Judaizers glorified in the marks of the flesh (i.e. circumcision) and put their reliance there.

3:21   Christ's power will bring everything under control.

4:1   'Stand firm' despite all the present struggles, all the attacks from heretics and those who oppose the gospel.

QUESTIONS

1. Look at the verbs Paul uses in 3:12-14. What do they tell us about Paul's view of the Christian life?

2. What are the 2 groups Paul describes in 3:2 and 3:18-19? How do they differ and how are they similar? Why would both groups be a danger to the church?

3. How does 3:20 help us to 'stand firm in the Lord' (4:1)?

FOCUS ACTIVITY

Perseverance   Divide the group into teams and give each team a blown up balloon. Place one half of each team at one end of the room and the remaining half at the other end of the room. On the command, 'Race!' the first member of each team runs to the other end of the room with a blown up balloon clenched between the knees. On arriving at the other end the balloon is handed to the next person who places the balloon between the knees and runs back to the other end of the room. The aim is to be the first team to change all its members from one end of the room to the other. The leader gives a running commentary, encouraging the teams to persevere.

In today's Bible study Paul uses a race to explain to the Philippians how they should live. Why might a race be a good metaphor to use? Let's see if you are right.

ACTIVITY

Photocopy page 53 for each group member. The letters in the shaded squares spell 'stand firm' (4:1).

Enter the following words into the grid, starting with the longest ones. When you have finished, rearrange the letters in the white circles to discover one of Paul's commands to the Philippians.

LORD	AWAIT	BODIES	CONTROL	GLORIOUS
MIND	CROSS	CHRIST	DESTINY	
	GLORY	HEAVEN	EAGERLY	TRANSFORM
	JESUS	THINGS	EARTHLY	
	OFTEN		ENABLES	CITIZENSHIP
	POWER		ENEMIES	DESTRUCTION
	SHAME		SAVIOUR	
	TEARS		STOMACH	

PREPARATION

Philippians 4:2-23

LESSON AIMS

To learn more of the all-sufficiency of Christ.

4:2 Paul is concerned for the unity of the church and this was one reason for the letter. We are not told the cause of the disagreement between the women, nor does Paul take sides, but he urges a fellow-worker to help them settle their differences.

4:4 'Rejoice' - a recurring theme in this letter. Paul has learnt the meaning of rejoicing despite outward circumstances precisely because it was 'in the Lord'.

4:6 Anxiety and prayer are in opposition to each other. Prayer can be made with thanksgiving because of the certainty that God meets needs even before they are spoken.

4:8 'True ... praiseworthy' - the list of virtues which should occupy a Christian's mind. What a person thinks about will be reflected in his deeds and words.

4:9 'Put into practice' - understanding the things learned or received is not to be confused with doing them.

4:10 'At last' - there may have been a problem with getting the gifts from the church to Paul, but eventually Epaphroditus had arrived and Paul was very appreciative (see v.18).

4:12 Contentment despite outward circumstances - cf. 1 Timothy 6:6.

4:16 Their giving to Paul had been on-going and generous.

4:19 'My God' - Paul's personal testimony.

4:20 Because of all that God meant to Paul he cannot but break out in a doxology.

4:22 Caesar's household - those in the employment of the Emperor, such as the palace guards.

QUESTIONS

1. Why was Paul so certain that Jesus would meet all his needs and those of the Philippians (v.13 and v.19)? Does this mean we can have everything we want?

2. If the Christian mind is so important how should we make use of TV, videos, books, etc?

FOCUS ACTIVITY

Chat Room Give each person a piece of paper and a pen and ask them to rate the following items from 0 to 10, where 10 = fantastic and 0 = awful.
How content are you with your:

sporting activity?	weight?	sex appeal?
family?	friends?	school work?
allowance / pocket money?		freedom?
prayer life?		

Reassure the group that no one will look at their paper - it is for their eyes only.

Once the group have completed their ratings, lead a discussion for a fixed time limit on whether or not they should be content with their current performance. Keep the discussion general and try to include everyone.

Paul had something to say to the Philippians regarding being content. Let's see what it was.

If we had been alive at the time of Paul and he had sent Timothy to find out about us (2:19), what sort of report would Timothy have taken back? Split the class into groups of 3/4 and get them to write a letter to the class from the apostle Paul. They are to write in **general** terms, not about individuals.

OVERVIEW
Taking the Gospel to the Greeks

Week 16	**Reaction to the Gospel**	*Acts 17:1-15*

To see the different reactions to the preaching of the gospel.

Week 17	**The Intellect and the Gospel**	*Acts 17:16-34*

To understand that the worldly view of intellect, and the value placed on it, is sometimes a hindrance to the gospel.

Week 18	**Persevering for the Gospel**	*Acts 18:1-22*

To learn the need to persevere in spite of hardships.

SERIES AIMS

1. To understand that people respond differently to hearing the gospel.

2. To learn that hardships are a normal part of gospel ministry.

MEMORY WORK

Do everything without complaining or arguing.
Philippians 2:14

Taking the Gospel to the Greeks

The previous series on Paul ended with him in Philippi. After leaving there Paul established the Macedonian churches of Thessalonica and Berea. He then journeyed on to Southern Greece (or Achaia) with his companions, visiting Athens and Corinth. Paul spent 18 months in the latter city, founding a church which would present him with many problems in the years to come. Through his co-workers, who included Doctor Luke, the writer of Acts, and by correspondence Paul kept in touch with the new churches in Macedonia. When Paul eventually left Corinth he spent a short time in Ephesus, where he left Priscilla and Aquila. From there he travelled to Jerusalem via Caesarea and then returned to Antioch.

For background information on Paul please see the series overview on page 19.

Paul's third missionary journey will be studied in Book 4.

PREPARATION

Acts 17:1-15

LESSON AIMS

To see the different reactions to the preaching of the gospel.

Sequence of events -

1. Paul and Silas left Philippi and went to Thessalonica where they stayed for at least 3 weeks, after which they were forced to leave by the Jews (see page 71). Since Timothy is not mentioned it is possible he stayed on in Philippi, joining Paul and Silas later in Berea (Acts 17:14).

2. Paul fled to Athens from Berea, leaving Silas and Timothy there.

3. Paul sent word back to Berea, instructing Silas and Timothy to join him as soon as possible.

4. Silas and Timothy must have rejoined Paul in Athens (see 1 Thessalonians 1:1; 3:1-2). Timothy was then sent back to Thessalonica to strengthen the new converts. Silas is not mentioned so it is possible he went back to Philippi when Timothy went to Thessalonica.

5. Paul went to Corinth where Silas and Timothy joined him. 1 Thessalonians was written from there, followed by 2 Thessalonians about 6 months later in AD 51/52.

17:1   The Egnatian Way crossed from east to west through present day northern Greece and was a major trade route. Philippi, Amphipolis and Thessalonica were on this route and were, therefore, strategic centres. It was estimated that a person would travel 30 miles a day, so each city would be about that distance apart. Thessalonica, about 100 miles from Philippi, was a busy seaport and capital of the province of Macedonia.

17:2   As usual, Paul visited the synagogue first.

17:4   Prominent women could mean the wives of leading men, or women who deserved notice in their own right.

17:5   Jealousy motivated the Jews' reaction (cf. 13:45), because of the response of the Greeks and the women.

17:7   'Defying Caesar's decrees' - to support a rival to Caesar was treason for a Roman.

17:9   'On bail' - Jason would have to guarantee to keep the peace or else he could forfeit his property or even his life.

17:10   No mention of Timothy. Berea is modern day Veroia, about 50 miles from Thessalonica.

17:13   The Jews again orchestrated trouble for Paul and Silas.

17:15   Athens, with its university, was still a leading city in Paul's day. Five centuries earlier it had been at its height of glory in art, philosophy, etc.

QUESTIONS

1. In Thessalonica and Berea Paul used the Scriptures (the OT) to explain the gospel. How did the hearers know he was speaking the truth? How should we react when people tell us about new doctrines?

2. Go through Acts 17:1-15 and note down the different reactions to the preaching of the gospel. What expectations should we have when telling others about the Lord Jesus?

VISUAL AID

Map - see page 22.

FOCUS ACTIVITY

Good Thing / Bad Thing   Ask group members to stand in the middle of the room. Explain that you are going to read out a list of words and you want them to react to those words. If the word is a good thing, they should move to the right of the room. If the word is a bad thing they should move to the left of the room. (If moving around the room is not easy, standing up or sitting down would give the same effect.) Tell the group to go with their 'gut' feeling and not to worry about what other people are doing.

Slowly read out the list below, giving people time to make their response and then return to the middle after each word.

> School
> Sport
> Exams
> Church
> Motorways
> Marmite
> Cycling
> Alarm clocks

(You may want to add to the list, but make sure you use words that will generate a variety of responses.)

Point out that different people react differently to different things. Let's find out how the people at Thessalonica reacted to Paul.

ACTIVITY

Photocopy page 60 for each group member.

Enter the 14 listed words into the word square. Each word reads in a straight line horizontally, vertically or diagonally and can read backwards or forwards. No letter is used more than once.

T	C	H	T	U	R	M	O	I	L	E	S
L	Y	H	E	X	S	J	T	A	M	I	I
U	N	E	R	K	D	E	T	O	L	H	E
A	E	S	E	I	C	W	R	A	I	U	J
P	I	E	P	Y	S	S	T	G	R	E	
U	R	R	E	S	H	T	E	O	V	E	A
G	R	Y	D	B	A	T	G	Y	G	T	L
O	S	E	E	I	A	O	N	F	W	O	
H	A	R	T	P	N	A	I	M	U	L	U
S	E	A	I	Y	D	K	W	A	I	S	S
A	T	R	S	U	C	R	O	W	D	T	E
A	C	I	N	O	L	A	S	S	E	H	T

BEREA

CHRIST

CROWD

GREEKS

JEALOUS

JEWS

KING

PAUL

RIOT

SILAS

SYNAGOGUE

THESSALONICA

TIMOTHY

TURMOIL

Now, starting from the top and reading from left to right, write down the remaining letters to discover what the people at Berea did.

PREPARATION

Acts 17:16-34

LESSON AIMS

To understand that the worldly view of intellect, and the value placed on it, is sometimes a hindrance to the Gospel.

17:16   Athens was a university city, but not the same glorious cultural centre as it was in the 4th century BC. It was a blend of superstition, idolatry and 'enlightened' philosophers.

17:17   Paul reasoned in the synagogue with the Jews and God-fearing Greeks, then in the market place, which was the general meeting place where people congregated for discussion. In this way he preached to the whole community.

17:18   Epicureans were philosophers who taught that it was unnecessary to seek after the gods. They held no fear of judgment, so everything was to be enjoyed for that moment.

Stoics were pantheistic, believing in the unity of mankind and kinship with the gods. They encouraged self-sufficiency and dogged endurance.

'Babbler' comes from the Greek word meaning a bird picking up seed - so an idler picking up scraps of information in the market place.

17:19   The Areopagus was the chief council in Athens in the 1st Century. It was held on the south side of the market place so was probably a public meeting.

17:22   'Religious' means superstitious.

17:23   'To an unknown God' - other Greek writers confirm that Athens at the time had altars with this inscription. The Greeks were fearful of offending a god by failing to pay him attention.

17:24   'The God who made the world' - this would conflict with the pantheistic belief of the Stoics.

17:26-27   'Made' ... 'determined' ... 'set for them' ... 'God planned and designed' - things were not left to chance as the Epicureans believed.

17:28   The 2 quotations from Greek poets show Paul's breadth of education. As an educated Roman he would have spoken Greek (the common language). This, together with his Jewish heritage, made him uniquely equipped to preach to all these races and cultures.

17:30-31   Paul points out that now they have heard the truth they can no longer claim ignorance and, as a result, are under God's judgment.

17:32   Although the Greeks believed in the immortality of the soul, the idea of a bodily resurrection was alien to their thinking.

17:33-34   Despite the scorn of some Greeks, Paul did gain some converts. Nothing definite is known about Dionysius, although later tradition turned him into the first bishop of Athens (a fair inference since the first converts often became the leaders of the church). It is doubtful that a church was formed at this stage because in 1 Corinthians 16:15 Paul describes the Corinthian converts as the first converts in Achaia.

QUESTIONS

1. The Athenians were superstitious. What is wrong with superstitions? Amongst your friends what superstitions are acted upon?

2. 1 Corinthians 1:23 speaks of how the gospel was so often received. Why can intellect be such a stumbling block to belief in Jesus?

3. How does the Bible define a fool? (Look up Psalm 14:1 and Proverbs 1:7 for help.)

Map - see page 22.

Obstacle Course   Create a simple obstacle course using tables and chairs. You can increase the element of risk by adding cups of water around the course. Divide the group into teams and run an obstacle relay race. The winner is the first team to finish.

Use the activity to introduce the idea of obstacles that get in the way. Let's see what obstacles Paul faced in Athens.

Photocopy page 63 for each group member. The place names are Athens, Berea, Corinth, Damascus, Ephesus, Jerusalem, Lystra, Rome, Tarsus, Thessalonica and Troas.

Unscramble these places connected with Paul's life and missionary journeys.

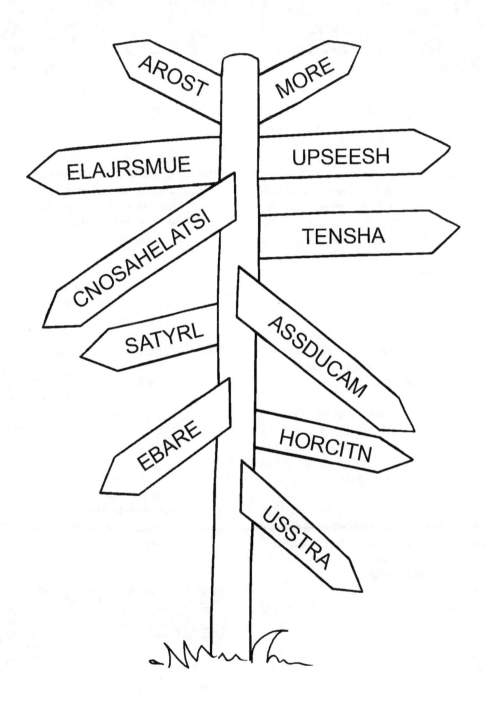

PREPARATION

Acts 18:1-22

LESSON AIMS

To learn the need to persevere in spite of hardships.

18:1 Corinth was an old Greek city which had been rebuilt by the Romans. It was strategically placed on a narrow neck of land between the Aegean and Adriatic Seas. It was a cosmopolitan city, a centre of trade and an obvious target for Paul; if a church was established here then Christianity would spread far and wide. But the town was a hard place for the gospel; it was dominated by a temple to Aphrodite (the goddess of love) and Corinth was a by-word for sexual immorality.

18:2 Aquila and Priscilla - since no mention is made here of their conversion it is likely that they were already Christians. They followed the same trade as Paul (tent making) and so they worked together (v.3).

Claudius issued an edict in about AD 49-50 expelling the Jews because of continual rioting 'instigated by Chrestus' (a common misspelling of Christ). This probably refers to a dispute between Christian and non-Christian Jews in Rome.

18:3 Tentmaker - Jewish custom provided manual training for sons from rich and poor families.

18:5-6 Paul preached to the Jews first.

18:7 Titius Justus would have been a God-fearing Gentile.

18:8 Crispus was a Jew, so the gospel had an effect on both groups.

18:12 Gallio was the brother of the famous philosopher, Seneca, the tutor of the future emperor Nero. He was the proconsul of Achaia in AD 51-52.

18:13 Judaisim was a legally recognised and licensed religion. The Jews were claiming that Paul was advocating an illegal religion.

18:14-15 Gallio was not impressed by their claims, and by dismissing the case he implicitly acknowledged that Paul's message was entitled to the same standing as other forms of Judaisim.

18:17 Sosthenes (cf. 1 Corinthians 1:1) was perhaps the second ruler of the synagogue to become a Christian in response to Paul's preaching (v.8).

18:18 'Some time' - 18 months (cf. v.11).

'vow he had taken' - probably a temporary Nazirite vow (Numbers 6:1-21). Different vows were taken to express thanks for deliverance and shaving the head marked a completion of the vow.

18:19 Ephesus was Paul's last port of call before returning home to Antioch via Caesarea and Jerusalem. He promised to return, God willing, and this he did on his 3rd missionary journey.

QUESTIONS

1. What encouragements and what discouragements did Paul have in Corinth? What experiences have encouraged or discouraged your faith?

VISUAL AID

Map - see page 22.

FOCUS ACTIVITY

Endurance Tests   Try some of the following endurance tests:

1. Get group members to stand with their arms outstretched at the side parallel to the ground. The winner is the one who can hold their arms out for the longest. This can be made harder by asking them to hold a book in each hand.

2. Get group members to lean against a wall with their legs at right angles. Again, the person who holds out the longest is the winner.

3. See who can hold their breath for the longest.

Comment on how hard it can be to keep going. Let's see how Paul managed to keep going in Corinth.

ACTIVITY

Today's activity is a game designed to revise both series on Paul. The game should be played in groups of 5-6. For each group photocopy page 66 at A3 size and glue onto card to make a board. Photocopy pages 67, 68 and 69 on card for each group and cut up to make a pack of question cards. Other requirements and the instructions for playing the game are written on page 66.

43	44 **Q**	45	46 **Q**	47	48 Athens was full of idols. Go back to square 32	49 **Back at Antioch**
42 **Q**	41	40 The people in Berea receive the gospel joyfully. Go forward 1 square	39 The Philippian jailer is converted. Go forward 2 squares.	38	37 **Q**	36
29 **Q**	30	31 Lydia is converted. Go forward 1 square	32	33 **Q**	34	35 Paul and Silas are put in prison. Go back 3 squares.
28	27 Timothy joins Paul and Silas. Go forward 3 squares.	26 Paul and Barnabas separate. Miss 1 turn.	25	24 **Q**	23	22 The Jews at Lystra stoned Paul. Go back 3 squares.
15	16 **Q**	17	18 John Mark deserts them. Go back to Jerusalem.	19	20 **Q**	21
14 God tells the church to set apart Paul and Barnabas for evangelism. Go forward 1 square	13	12 **Q**	11	10 **Q**	9	8 Paul leaves Damascus in fear of his life. Miss 1 turn.
1 **Jerusalem**	2	3 Paul persecutes the Christians. Go back 1 square.	4	5 **Q**	6	7 Paul is converted on the road to Damascus. Go forward 2 squares.

Required

Counters for each player.
1 dice.
1 pack of Question cards (shuffled).

Instructions

1. Throw the dice to decide who starts - the person who throws the highest number.

2. The play then moves in a clockwise direction.

3. Each player throws the dice and moves the number thrown. If he/she lands on a square with instructions written on it, these instructions must be obeyed. If he/she lands on a square with **Q** written on it, one of the other players takes the top question card and reads out the question.

If the player answers correctly he/she moves forward 1 square.

For an incorrect answer the player moves backwards 1 square.

4. The first player to reach square 49 **"back at Antioch"**, wins.

NB for the teacher

This game is for revision of the two Paul series. If an incorrect answer is given, see if any other player knows the answer. (A correct answer from another player does not result in that player's counter moving forward.)

Q Why was Paul going to Damascus?

A To arrest the Christians.

Q How did Paul change when he became a Christian?

A Instead of persecuting the church he preached the gospel.

Q What were Paul and Barnabas doing when God told the church to send them on their first journey?

A fasting and praying.

Q What was the first place Paul visited on arrival in a new town?

A The synagogue.

Q Why did Paul and Barnabas separate?

A Barnabas wanted to take John Mark and Paul did not because John Mark had left them previously.

Q Where was Paul going when he saw a bright light?

A Damascus

Q To what group of people beginning with G did God call Paul to take the gospel?

A Gentiles

Q What was the name of Paul's companion on his first journey?

A Barnabas

Q In Cyprus, a magician tried to stop the Governor hearing about Jesus. What happened to him?

A He was made blind.

Q Can you name one of the places Paul visited on his first journey?

A Cyprus, Antioch in Pisidia, Iconium, Lystra, Derbe.

Q What was Paul's name before he was converted?

A Saul

Q What was the name of the man God sent to help Paul receive his sight?

A Ananias

Q How did Paul escape from Damascus?

A He was let down the wall in a basket

Q Who went with Paul and Barnabas on their first journey and later turned back?

A John Mark

Q What 2 things happened each time Paul preached the gospel?

A Some believed but others opposed him

Q Who does Paul take with him on his second journey?

A Silas

Q What strange thing happened at Philippi?

A A slave girl with an evil spirit followed them around. Paul cast out the spirit.

Q Who was converted at Philippi as a result of Paul and Silas being imprisoned?

A The jailer.

Q What was the false teaching that was discussed at the Council of Jerusalem?

A The need for Gentile Christians to be circumcised.

Q Where did Lydia come from?

A Thyatira

Q Whom do Paul and Silas meet in Lystra and take with them?

A Timothy

Q Why did Paul get put in prison at Philippi?

A He cast out the evil spirit from the slave girl, which meant she could not earn money by fortune telling.

Q In Berea, how did the people check that Paul was telling the truth?

A They searched the Scriptures.

Q After Paul left Philippi which major town did he visit?

A Thessalonica

Q Who, with his entire household, believed in the Lord at Corinth?

A Crispus, the ruler of the synagogue.

Q How did Paul know God wanted him to go to Greece?

A He had a vision of a man saying, "Come and help us."

Q What were Paul and Silas doing in prison when the earthquake occurred?

A Singing hymns and praying.

Q In which city did Paul see lots of idols?

A Athens

Q Who did Paul meet at Corinth?

A Priscilla and Aquila.

Q What does Hebrews 12:10 say?

A God disciplines us for our good, that we may share in his holiness.

Q What does Philippians 2:14 say?

A Do everything without complaining or arguing.

Q Give the Bible reference for -
God disciplines us for our good, that we may share in his holiness.

A Hebrews 12:10

Q Give the Bible reference for -
Do everything without complaining or arguing.

A Philippians 2:14

OVERVIEW
1 Thessalonians

Week 19

Thanksgiving   *1 Thessalonians 1:1-10*
To discover the state of the church at Thessalonica.

Week 20

Paul's Example   *1 Thessalonians 2:1-16*
To understand that our lives must back up our message.

Week 21

Care and Concern   *1 Thessalonians 2:17 - 3:13*
To learn how Paul cared for the new church and how we should care for one another.

Week 22

The God-Pleasing Life   *1 Thessalonians 4:1-12*
To learn how we should live as Christians.

Week 23

The Second Coming   *1 Thessalonians 4:13 - 5:11*
To learn about the second coming of Christ and how we should live in the light of it.

Week 24

Final Instructions   *1 Thessalonians 5:12-28*
To learn how we should live as members of the Christian community.

SERIES AIMS

1. To understand Paul's teaching about Christian living in the light of the second coming of Christ.

2. To apply those teachings to our own lives.

MEMORY WORK

May the Lord strengthen your hearts so that you will be blameless and holy in the presence of our God and Father when our Lord Jesus comes with all his holy ones.

1 Thessalonians 3:13

1 Thessalonians

Having just completed the series on the final stages of Paul's second missionary journey, the group should know about Paul's visit to Thessalonica and understand something about the needs of the early church in that city. Thessalonica was a free city and the capital of the Roman province of Macedonia. It was a prosperous seaport and was on the main trade route from Istanbul. It was also an important communication and trading centre, being located at the junction of the Egnatian Way and the road leading north to the Danube. The city had a population of about 200,000, making it the largest city in Macedonia. Since Paul began his ministry in the Jewish synagogue (Acts 17:1-9) it is reasonable to assume that the new church included some Jews, but 1 Thessalonians 1:9-10 and Acts 17:4 indicate a large Gentile membership.

Background from Acts -

1. Paul and Silas left Philippi and went to Thessalonica where they stayed for possibly around 3 weeks, after which they were forced to leave by the Jews. Some commentators suggest a longer time gap between Acts 17:4 and 17:5, because 3 weeks seems very short for such a strong church to be founded (see also Philippians 4:16). Since Timothy is not mentioned it is possible he stayed on in Philippi, joining Paul and Silas later in Berea (Acts 17:14).

2. Paul fled to Athens from Berea, leaving Silas and Timothy there.

3. Paul sent word back to Berea, instructing Silas and Timothy to join him as soon as possible.

4. Silas and Timothy must have rejoined Paul in Athens (see 1 Thessalonians 1:1; 3:1-2). Timothy was then sent back to Thessalonica to strengthen the new converts. Silas is not mentioned so it is possible he went back to Philippi when Timothy went to Thessalonica.

5. Paul went to Corinth where Silas and Timothy joined him. 1 Thessalonians was written from there, followed by 2 Thessalonians about 6 months later in AD 51/52.

The first letter is generally dated as AD 51 and is one of Paul's earliest letters to the churches. (Some commentators suggest that Galatians may have been written earlier in approximately AD 48-49 shortly before the committee of enquiry met at Jerusalem to resolve the issue of the need for Christians to be circumcised (Acts 15:1-2).) It was written to encourage the early church in its trials and to reassure them about their future in Christ.

When Paul fled from Thessalonica after his brief stay, new converts from paganism were left at a time of persecution with little support. Paul wrote to encourage the Christians in their difficulties (1 Thessalonians 3:3-5), to give instructions about living as a Christian (4:1-8) and to reassure them of the certainty of Christ's second coming. The latter runs throughout the letter; every chapter ends with a reference to it and chapter 4 majors on the theme.

PREPARATION

1 Thessalonians 1:1-10

LESSON AIMS

To discover the state of the church at Thessalonica.

1:1 Paul, Silas and Timothy were the 3 founder members of the church. Silas was a leader in the church at Jerusalem and was chosen by that church to go with Paul and Barnabas to Antioch to report the church's decision regarding what was required for Gentile converts to be accepted into fellowship (Acts 15:22-23). Following his disagreement with Barnabas over John Mark, Paul chose Silas to be his travelling companion (Acts 15:36-41). Silas was a Roman citizen and a prophet (Acts 15:32).

Timothy was a native of Lystra, in modern day Turkey, and was from a mixed background, with a Greek father and a mother who was a Jewish Christian (Acts 16:1). Paul invited him to go with him and Silas on his second missionary journey. Prior to their setting out Paul circumcised Timothy so that his Greek heritage would not be a hindrance (Acts 16:3). Silas and Timothy accompanied Paul through Macedonia and Achaia, so both were known to the Thessalonians.

The church was not a building, but a group of believers meeting in one another's homes. 'In God …' speaks of the church being under God's authority and in close relationship with him.

1:2 'Thank God for all of you' - this is a customary opening remark of Paul's, showing his love and concern for the church.

1:3 The 3 foundational Christian qualities of faith, love and hope are cited by Paul as the reason for their hard work and endurance. For faith, love and hope cf. 1 Corinthians 13:13. For faith shown in action cf. James 2:14-17.

1:4 The reasons for Paul's conviction about the genuineness of the Thessalonians' faith are stated in verses 5-10.

1:5 'Our gospel' - the only one that Paul preached, but it is God's Gospel (2:8) and also Christ's (3:2).

Without the power of the Holy Spirit human words are useless.

1:6-7 Imitators and models - the example set by first Paul and then the church members was of the utmost importance in the spread of the gospel. (As yet there was very little in the way of New Testament writings).

Greece was divided into the 2 provinces of Macedonia and Achaia.

1:8 'Everywhere' - a general term for all the places where Christians were to be found. Remember that this letter was only written a few months after the church was founded.

1:9-10 Three marks of their conversion -
- ◆ turning to God from idols
- ◆ serving God
- ◆ waiting for Christ's return.

QUESTIONS

1. How did Paul demonstrate his concern for the believers in Thessalonica?

2. What evidence is there in this passage that God was at work?

3. How had the Thessalonians changed since becoming Christians?

VISUAL AID

See map on page 22.

FOCUS ACTIVITY

Who is it?   Divide the group into teams and give each team a list of 3 or 4 well-known figures, present day or historical. The team has 5 minutes to work out 5 statements that build into a description of each person on their list. Teams take it in turns to describe one person, starting with the first statement. After each statement the remaining teams have a chance to guess who is being described. An accurate guess after 1 statement earns that team 5 points, with the points decreasing for each additional statement. An accurate guess after all 5 statements earns that team 1 point. The leader acts as referee.

Point out how difficult it can be to guess the person described when only given very limited information. Let's see what we can find out about the Thessalonian Christians from Paul's description of them.

ACTIVITY

Photocopy page 74 for each person.

There are no clues to this puzzle. First crack the code with the help of the given letters. Each small number refers to a specific letter. When you have finished, the shaded words will complete the Bible verse at the foot of the page.

7	11	4	17	24	2		23	14	13	9	1	2
14		17	15	14	24		16			15		22
16	14	17	1		17	11	4	2	14	9		13
21		4			11		26	15	9	11		4
		21	14	13	9	8	11	17		2		17
8	14		18		8		16				26	11
4			18	4	24	7	11	17		20	11	
5	4	9	15	2	7		2	4	16	4	1	
11			19		11	4	2	21		9	15	10
		3	15	16	9	2					19	
15	1	11	4			10	4	9		25	4	20
24		8	16	4	12	11		11		4	16	11
11					14	9	21	6		10		9
26	15	6		2	14			24 T	17 R	11 E	4	24

1	2	3	4	5	6	7	8	9	10	11 E	12	13
14	15	16	17 R	18	19	20	21	22	23	24 T	25	26

May the .... your .... so that you will be

.... and .... in the presence of our God and

.... when our Lord Jesus comes with all his holy ones.

From which verse in 1 Thessalonians 3 does this come?

PREPARATION

1 Thessalonians
2:1-16

LESSON AIMS

To understand that our lives must back up our message.

This passage is about Paul - how his message was validated by his life (v.1-12) and by its result (v.13-16). Many itinerant religious and philosophical teachers travelled around living off their hearers, so it was important for Paul to make clear that he was different from the others.

2:1   'You know' - Paul appeals to the believers' personal knowledge of events.

Paul's visit to Thessalonica had not been a failure (see v.13).

2:2   See Acts 16:19-40.

2:3   The Greek word used for 'trick' meant the lure for catching fish.

2:4   Paul's motive for preaching was to please God, not men.

'Hearts' does not refer only to emotions, but also includes intellects and wills. The 'heart' is the control centre of the personality, the place where decisions are made.

2:5-6   Paul's aim was never for personal profit nor was he seeking praise from men.

2:6   Apostles were entitled to support from the church (see 1 Corinthians 9:3-14).

2:9   Paul had probably worked as a tentmaker in his desire to show love and not to be a burden on the fledgling congregation (Acts 18:3). The Greeks despised manual work, viewing it as only fit for slaves, but Paul was not ashamed of doing it in order to further the cause of the gospel.

2:10-12   Paul appeals to the Thessalonians' own experience regarding the blamelessness of the missionaries' lives (cf. Ephesians 4:1).

2:13   The Thessalonians had recognised the gospel as being the word of God and having authority.

2:14   Paul encourages the Christians that suffering is a mark of the true church and not a sign that something has gone wrong. The Thessalonians suffered under the hands of their countrymen (Acts 17:5-9), just as the church in Jerusalem had suffered under the hands of the Jews.

2:15-16   Hindering the spread of the gospel leads to experiencing God's wrath. Paul speaks of this in the present tense, either because it had already been partially experienced by the Jews or because of its absolute certainty.

QUESTIONS

1. From this passage list all the accusations that had been levelled at Paul. How does he justify himself?

2. In what ways did Paul show the gospel to the Thessalonians? How should this affect the way I relate to the people at school?

3. How does this passage illustrate the truth of Matthew 7:20?

Words and Actions   The aim is to see if words are backed up by actions. Divide the group into 2 teams. One member of each team comes out and is asked how many times they can head a football without it falling to the ground. Both team members state how many times they can do it. The one who states the least number is given the opportunity to increase their number. Carry on until both have reached their highest number. The person who states the highest number is asked to do it. If he completes the task successfully his team wins a point. If he fails the opposing team get a point. Continue as time allows, using different team members each time.
Suggested tasks:

◆   how many goes to burst a balloon (least number wins)
◆   how many plastic cups to build a tower
◆   how many balls can be thrown into a bucket in 10 goes
◆   how many songs by a specific pop group can be named
◆   how many football teams in a specific division can be named.

Did their actions back up their words? Comment on the need for actions to back up words if the team was to be successful. Let's see what Paul had to say about this when people in Thessalonica questioned the validity of his ministry.

Photocopy page 77 for each person. 'Approved' is the word left in the grid after completing the word search.   It comes from 1 Thessalonians 2:4.

All the following words from the Bible passage can be found in letter pairs in the grid. The words read in a straight line either horizontally, vertically or diagonally and can read backwards or forwards, but the letter pairs will always read from left to right. No letter pair is used more than once. One word on the list has been done to show you. When you have found all the listed words you will be left with a word that tells us what God thought of Paul.

APOSTLES	COUNTRYMEN	IMPURE	PROPHETS
APPEAL	DEAR	HOLY	PREACHED
BELIEVED	FLATTERY	INSULTED	RECEIVED
BROTHERS	GENTLE	LORD	SINS
BURDEN	GOSPEL	MASK	SUFFERED
CHILDREN	HARDSHIP	MOTHER	TOIL
CHURCHES	HEARTS	OPPOSITION	WORD
COMFORTING	HELP	PRAISE	WORTHY

ON	TI	SI	PO	OP	SU	ED	LO	IN	RS
PR	RD	GO	TO	IL	OV	FF	SU	RD	HE
EA	IP	WO	SP	PR	ES	LT	ER	CH	OT
CH	SH	SE	AP	EL	ED	TL	UR	ED	BR
ED	RD	AI	TS	CO	AP	CH	OS	HO	LY
HE	HA	PR	MF	HE	ES	PE	ED	AP	FL
NS	AR	OR	AR	DE	OP	IV	AL	AT	CH
SI	TI	TS	BE	GE	CE	PR	TE	RE	IL
NG	LP	LI	EN	RE	NT	RY	MA	PU	DR
HE	EV	RD	MO	TH	ER	LE	SK	IM	EN
ED	BU	EN	YM	TR	UN	CO	WO	RT	HY

What is the remaining word and which verse is it from?

PREPARATION

1 Thessalonians
2:17 - 3:13

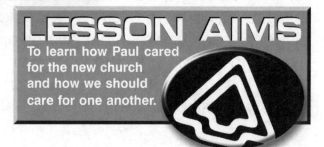

LESSON AIMS

To learn how Paul cared for the new church and how we should care for one another.

2:17   Paul had left Thessalonica earlier than he had planned.

2:18   It may be that Paul had been forbidden to return, following the trouble he had with the city rulers (Acts 17:5-9).

2:19   The crown does not refer to a royal crown but to the wreath used on festive occasions or as the victor's garland in Greek games.

3:1   The 'we' is an editorial one, referring to Paul alone.

3:3-4   Paul reassures the Thessalonians that their trials are not to be marvelled at, but expected.

3:5   Timothy was sent to see if the Thessalonians were standing firm. Belief in the power of God to preserve his people did not prevent Paul from feeling concern for the young Christians and did not stop him praying for them.

3:6   Paul rejoices in the good news Timothy has brought back from Thessalonica. The good news is threefold - their faith, love and longing to see Paul.

3:9   Paul could have congratulated himself on work well done, but instead gives all the glory to God.

3:10   Although the Thessalonians were standing firm and an example to other churches (1:7-8), they were not perfect in either Christian knowledge or behaviour. In this letter Paul gives them in writing what he had been unable to give them in person. At the time of writing he was praying and longing for the opportunity to visit them again. This prayer was answered during his third missionary journey (Acts 20:1-3).

QUESTIONS

1. What was Paul's prayer for the Thessalonians? (3:9-13)

2. What practical steps can we take to increase our love for each other? (v.12)

3. What incentive does Paul give for holy living? (v.13)

FOCUS ACTIVITY

Care and Concern   Divide the group into teams and give each team two rolls of toilet paper. Inform the teams that one of their members has had a road accident resulting in multiple fractures. They must show their care and concern by bandaging the injured person with the toilet paper. Judge the efforts.

In today's Bible passage we will see how Paul showed his care and concern for the Thessalonians.

ACTIVITY

Divide into small groups and give each group the following scenarios to discuss:

1. John is living with his parents in a country where the government is opposed to Christian teaching. His parents are medical missionaries and are supported by your church. He has written to the group to tell them about the hardships his family are undergoing because they are Christians. They have heard about another missionary family that was attacked by a mob and badly hurt and are afraid that the same thing may happen to them. John has to be driven to and from school because it is not safe for him to walk on his own. How can you show support for John?

2. Jenny is a member of your youth group and is feeling very depressed. She has moved to a new school and is finding it difficult to make friends. During a recent lesson the teacher commented that no one believes the Bible anymore. Jenny took her courage in both hands and said that she did. The class laughed. Since then Jenny has been teased unkindly about her Christian stance. How can you help Jenny and show her how much you care?

Get feedback from the groups if time permits.

PREPARATION

1 Thessalonians 4:1-12

LESSON AIMS

To learn how we should live as Christians.

4:1-2 The reason for living an ethical life is to please God. This instruction comes with God's authority, so it is not an option.

4:3 Sanctification is the ongoing process of becoming more like Jesus.

4:3-8 The first issue Paul raises is freedom from sexual immorality. This needed emphasising because the highest pagan ethic fell far short of the Jewish and Christian standard. Sexual immorality refers to any form of sexual intercourse outside heterosexual marriage.

4:6 By committing adultery the person is breaking up the marriage relationship and thus wronging his brother.

4:6-7 These verses state God's view of sexual immorality.

4:8 God gives his Holy Spirit to enable us to live holy lives. If we reject his instructions we are rejecting him.

4:9-10 Love for fellow believers is another mark of the God-pleasing life.

4:11 These 3 commands deal with things that are potentially disruptive to the church fellowship. To lead a quiet life is not to be argumentative. Mind your own business means do not gossip. Work with your own hands refers to earning your own living. Some members of the church were so taken up with the second coming of Christ that they had stopped concerning themselves with earning their living and were sponging off fellow Christians. That this was an ongoing problem is seen in 2 Thessalonians 3:6-10.

4:12 Respect from the unbeliever is the result of living a God-pleasing life.

QUESTIONS

1. People today tend to view morality as relative. What does Paul say in this passage about that viewpoint?

2. Does it matter if my belief system is divorced from my behaviour?

3. How can we put verse 11 into practice?

FOCUS ACTIVITY

Helpful Hints What instructions would you send to a group of 11 year olds, who are about to come up to High School, to help them settle in quickly? Divide the group into threes or fours and give them 5 minutes to come up with a set of easily understood instructions. At the end of the time ask for feedback from the groups and judge which group has done the best.

Let's see what instructions Paul gave to the Thessalonians about how they should behave as Christians.

ACTIVITY

Photocopy page 81 for each group member. The shaded squares spell, 'Respect of outsiders' (v.12).

In this passage Paul gives the Thessalonians instructions on how to live as Christians. Enter every word of the Bible verse below into the crossword grid. Underline each word as you position it. When you have finished rearrange the letters in the shaded squares to spell one of the results of a God-pleasing life.

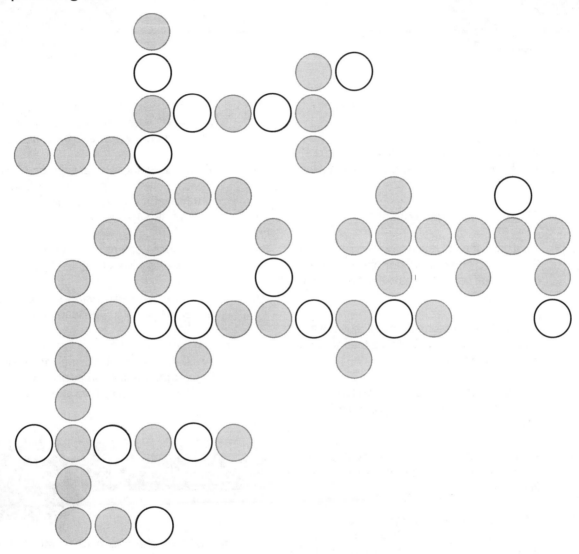

Finally, brothers, we instructed you how to live in order to please God, as in fact you are living.

1 Thessalonians 4:1

The _ _ _ _ _ _ _ of _ _ _ _ _ _ _ _ _

WEEK 23
The Second Coming

PREPARATION

1 Thessalonians
4:13 - 5:11

LESSON AIMS

To learn about the second coming of Christ and how we should live in the light of it.

Since Paul left Thessalonica 2 questions about the second coming had arisen -

1. Would those people who had already died lose out?
2. When was Jesus returning and was it worth planning for the future?

4:13-18 Those who had already died.

4:13 Paul gives the first reason for teaching about the second coming - to remove ignorance so that the Thessalonians will not grieve like unbelievers.

4:14 The death and resurrection of Jesus are the reason we can believe Paul's teaching on the second coming.

4:15 This is backed up by Jesus' own teaching - 'the Lord's own word' (see Matthew 24:30-31).

4:16 Reassurance that those already dead will not miss out - 'the dead in Christ will rise first'.

4:17 'Meet' signifies the meeting or 'audience' with a great king or governor. When such a one approached a city the population and/or council would go out to meet him and escort him into the city.

4:18 The second reason for teaching about the second coming - as an encouragement (see also 5:11).

5:1-11 These verses answer the second question (see left) - was it possible for Christians to be caught unawares and thus miss out?

5:1-3 Paul's teaching was always practical and never to satisfy idle curiosity. No one knows when Jesus will come again (cf. Matthew 24:3-14,36-44).

5:4-5 The Thessalonians will not be caught out if they live holy lives (see 4:1-12).

5:6 'Others, who are asleep' refers to the unbelievers, not to the dead in Christ (4:14-15; 5:10).

5:8 As Christians, we live in the light, so will not be caught out like the pagan, who lives in the darkness. Faith, love and hope - cf. 1:2-3.

QUESTIONS

1. Does Paul's teaching in 4:13-18 mean that we should not grieve following the death of a Christian? (See also John 11:33-38.)

2. What practical changes should we make in the way we should live while waiting for Christ's return?

Truth or Rumour? Divide the group into pairs. Place the partners on opposite sides of the room, using all four sides so that people are evenly spaced around the room. Give one member of each pair a newspaper cutting and the other member a pen and paper. The newspaper cuttings should be of similar length and there should be at least 6 different ones for a group of 12 or over. The people with the newspaper cuttings shout them out to their partners, who try and record them on paper. After a set period of time ask the transcribers to read out what they have written. The winning pair is the one who most successfully records the newspaper cutting.

Point out how difficult it was to distinguish what was being said. Those who did not hear properly did not write the correct words. The Thessalonians had misunderstood some of Paul's teaching and this was causing problems. Let's see what the problem was and how Paul answered their concerns.

This activity is designed to get the events of Jesus' second coming into the correct order. Divide into small groups and either write a newspaper article or produce a television news report based on the Bible passage. Give the groups 10-15 minutes to work on their project. If there is insufficient time to show the other groups what they have done, this could be done as a lead in activity next time.

PREPARATION

1 Thessalonians
5:12-28

LESSON AIMS

To learn how we should live as members of the Christian community.

5:12   These verses are addressed to fellow Christians - 'brothers'.

5:12-15   The first instructions are to do with the Christian's relationships with those in the church.

5:12   This verse describes the elders.

5:13   'Live in peace' - cf. 4:11.

5:14   Some commentators suggest that 'brothers' in this verse refers to the elders, not to all the Christians as in v.12.

    'Warn those who are idle' - cf. 4:11-12.

5:16-18   These verses deal with the Christian's relationship with God.

5:19-22   The gift of prophecy. Prophets declared God's word to the people. The true prophet was recognised by his words coming true (1 Kings 17:22-24).

5:19-20   Paul calls on the Thessalonians to recognise the gift of prophecy and not disregard it.

5:21-22   However, they were not to take prophecies at face value, but to test them to make sure they were from God, i.e. that they agreed with what God said in Scripture. Anything that is not from God is bad and is to be jettisoned or avoided.

5:23-24   Sanctification is an ongoing process and, although human effort is required, it comes about through God's faithfulness. These verses are not suggesting sinless perfection this side of heaven.

QUESTIONS

1. Discuss who is referred to in verse 12. What does it mean to respect these people? How does this work out in practice and does it only apply to church matters?

2. How should we deal with differences of opinion within the fellowship?

3. How can we put into practice verses 16-18?

FOCUS ACTIVITY

Working Together   Divide into roughly equal teams of at least 6 people. Apart from the person at the head, the members of each team form a chain by holding onto the waist of the person in front. The person at the back of each chain tucks a coloured piece of paper or cloth into his belt to form a tail. On the word, 'Go!' each team tries to grab the tail from the other teams without losing their own. Only the head of the chain is allowed to grab.

Comment on the need to work as a team if the chain was to succeed. Let's see what Paul had to say to the Thessalonians about working together in the church.

A quiz to revise the series. Divide the group into 2 teams. The winner is the first team to collect 6 smiley faces (see diagram).

Requirements
Each team requires a set of 8 faces, 6 with smiles and 2 with sad mouths. The faces are randomly numbered from 1-8 on the back and are pinned to the board with the numbers showing. The sad faces introduce an element of luck so that a team member who answers a question incorrectly will not place their team in an irretrievable position. Prepare 16 questions to bring out the main points from the series.

Rules
A question is put to each team in turn and, if answered correctly, one of the team members chooses a face by calling out its number. The face is turned over and, if a smiley one, is left on the board. A sad face is removed from the board. If an incorrect answer is given the question is offered to the other team. Allow 10 minutes for the quiz.

PREPARATION

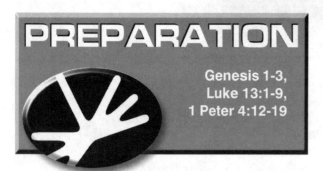

Genesis 1-3,
Luke 13:1-9,
1 Peter 4:12-19

LESSON AIMS

To understand the reason why suffering is present in our world and how the Christian should respond to it.

As with all the apologetics lessons, the information in these notes is to be assimilated by the teacher, who can then decide on an appropriate presentation to the group. The topic may have been looked at by the group a couple of years ago when studying Job (On the Way for 9-11s, Book 6 weeks 13 & 14). The notes follow a suggested approach, but you may want to vary it with your group.

Introduction
1. Define suffering - pain, loss, grief, defeat, change, punishment, wrong, etc. This can manifest itself in several ways - emotional, physical, mental or spiritual.

2. Divide the group into pairs. Give each pair a newspaper and a pair of scissors. Ask them to go through the newspaper and cut out any articles which show some sort of suffering, either at home or abroad. Try and give each pair a different newspaper. For a large group it might be necessary to split newspapers between pairs.

3. Ask for feedback from the group and write their answers on a flip chart. Categorise their answers, aiming to get the following:

disease	job loss	divorce
famine	war	cruelty
guilt	poverty	bereavement
broken friendships	natural disasters	

The Problem
1. If God is good and God is powerful why are innocent people allowed to suffer?

2. Why doesn't God do something to stop wars, famines, etc?

How suffering came into the world   Genesis 1-3
In the Bible suffering is regarded as an intrusion into the created world. From Genesis ch. 1-3 we learn:

1:31   When God finished creation it was all very good.

1:26   Man was special in that he was made in God's image.

1:26-28   Man was given authority to rule over creation. God blessed man, made him to be fruitful and commanded him to subdue the earth.

2:15   Man was given work.

2:17   Man was given free will. This meant that God did not control him like a robot but allowed him to choose to obey God.

2:18   Man was given a helper.

3:8   The Garden of Eden was not just a nice place to live, it was also the place where God walked, so Adam and Eve were living in the presence of God.

What did man do with free will? He rebelled against God. Instead of serving God he wanted to do things his way and make himself the most important person. Because the man and woman rebelled against God, he cursed them. The blessings God gave them were all changed.

3:17-18   No longer was all creation good. The ground was cursed and started to grow thistles and weeds.

3:19   Death entered the world. No longer was man to be like God and live for ever.

3:16-18   No longer was man blessed by God. God cursed Adam and Eve and they were no longer able to subdue the earth.

3:17   Work became hard; it was no longer a blessing.

3:16   Adam and Eve no longer lived in harmony. Relationship problems would develop.

3:23   Man was banished from God's presence. No longer were they able to talk with God in the garden.

When he was banished from the presence of God man became utterly selfish. The one blessing not taken away from him was free will. Man was allowed to continue in his rebellion. So, when Adam and Eve rebelled against God, the good world that God had created changed for ever. Paul, in his letter to Roman Christians, described creation as 'groaning' and 'in bondage to decay' (Romans 8:18-22). Since the Fall there has been something terribly wrong with man and also with creation.

How do these curses relate to the human suffering we see today?

On the board/flip chart match up the following with the items written down in the introduction:

relationship problems   ground cursed
work became hard   unable to subdue the earth
death   man utterly selfish
banished from God's presence.

Is suffering always a direct result of sin? Luke 13:1-9

From Genesis 1-3 we see that all suffering is a result of the entry of sin into the world. However, Scripture does not teach that a person's suffering is a direct result of his sin.

13:1   Some pilgrims had come from Galilee to Jerusalem to celebrate the Passover. Whilst slaughtering their sacrifices they were killed by Roman soldiers.

13:2   Orthodox Jews believed that suffering a major calamity indicated how great a sinner the person was (see also John 9:2).

13:3   Jesus pointed out that the whole Jewish nation were sinners and liable for judgment (see also v.5).

13:4   The Tower of Siloam was built inside the south eastern section of the wall of Jerusalem.

13:6-9   The fig tree symbolises the nation of Israel. Judgment will come one day, but God was giving them a further chance to repent. If they refused, they would have brought judgment on themselves.

India is in a chronic state of famine, yet the people grow sufficient grain to feed the entire population. The majority of Indians are Hindu and believe all animal life is sacred. As a result, rats are not killed, but allowed to breed unchecked. Rats eat grain and the people starve.

Why doesn't God do anything about the suffering in the world?

1. He has given man free will. Romans 1:28-32 says that God has given man over to his sin - he lets man get on with it.

2. He can work his purposes through it. Suffering often makes people see their need of God. It also acts like a refining fire in the lives of those who do know God, making them more like Christ (James 1:2-4, 1 Peter 1:6-7).

3. One day God will do something (Revelation 21:3-4) - but he will come in judgment and it will then be too late for men to repent.

4. God is patiently waiting because of his great love for all men. Do we really want God to come in judgment today?

Suffering as a Christian   1 Peter 4:12-19

In the same way that man rebels against God and hates him, man also hates those who follow God and bear his 'stamp' as Christians (John 15:20).

4:12   Suffering is a trial - a test to prove the reality of faith. It is nothing surprising, but is to be expected.

4:13   We should rejoice that we are being identified with Christ.

4:14   Suffering brings the opportunity to prove God's faithfulness through the presence of his Holy Spirit.

4:15   A warning not to attribute suffering for our own misdeeds to suffering as a Christian.

4:17   A challenge to prove the relevance of the gospel as judgment begins with the people of God. If Christians were immune from suffering what relevance would they have as they take the gospel to their unbelieving neighbours?

4:19   Suffering brings an opportunity to commit ourselves to God and to prove his faithfulness.

The eternal perspective

If this life is all there is it would be unfair. However, if God uses suffering to show people their need of him, they are in some senses more privileged than those who never see their need. We know that when Jesus comes again all wrongs will be righted (2 Thessalonians 1:5-10).

Questions

Try to refer back to the notes on the board/flip chart when answering questions.

Further reading

The Problem of Pain by C.S. Lewis
A Grief Observed by C.S. Lewis

Bible Timeline

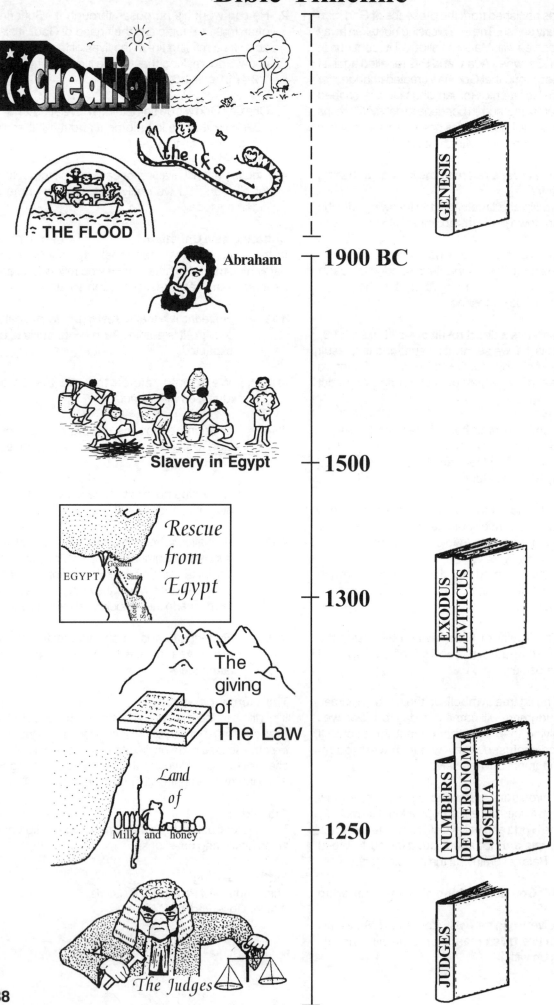

Creation

THE FLOOD

Abraham

1900 BC

Slavery in Egypt

1500

Rescue from Egypt

EGYPT   Goshen   Sinai   Red Sea

1300

The giving of The Law

Land of Milk and honey

1250

The Judges

GENESIS

EXODUS   LEVITICUS

NUMBERS   DEUTERONOMY   JOSHUA

JUDGES

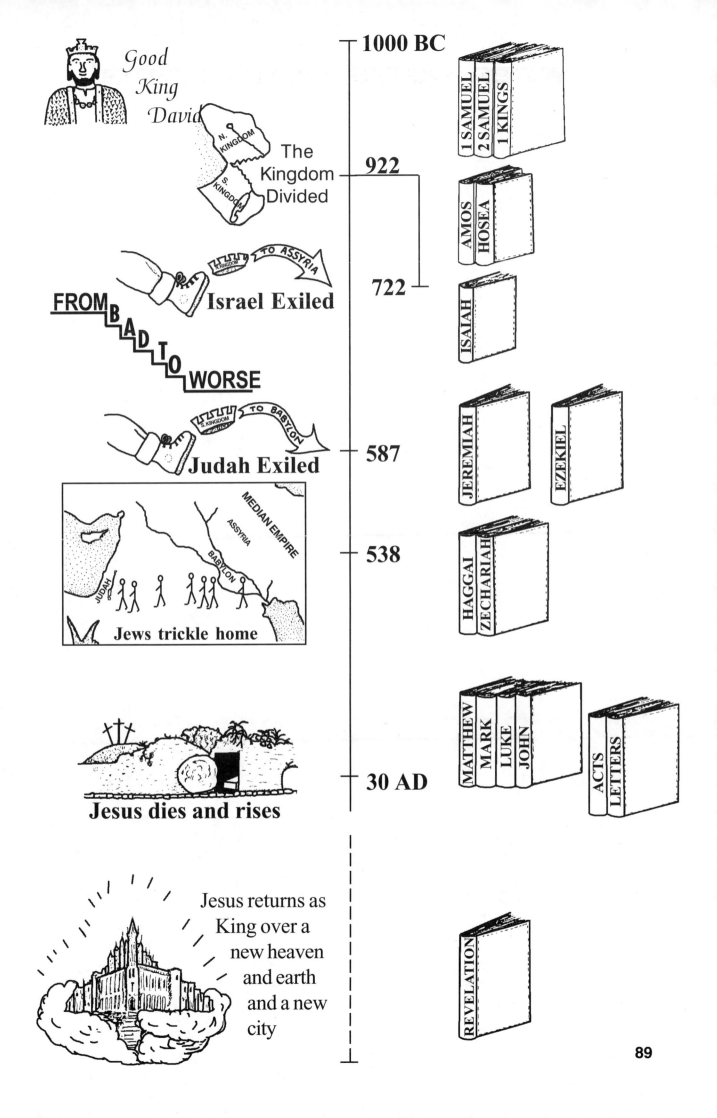

Good King David

The Kingdom Divided

FROM BAD TO WORSE

Israel Exiled

Judah Exiled

Jews trickle home

Jesus dies and rises

Jesus returns as King over a new heaven and earth and a new city

1000 BC

922

722

587

538

30 AD

1 SAMUEL 2 SAMUEL 1 KINGS

AMOS HOSEA

ISAIAH

JEREMIAH EZEKIEL

HAGGAI ZECHARIAH

MATTHEW MARK LUKE JOHN ACTS LETTERS

REVELATION

NOTES NOTES NOTES NOTES

NOTES NOTES NOTES NOTES

NOTES NOTES NOTES NOTES

NOTES NOTES NOTES NOTES

The Game is Up
OLD TESTAMENT

Book 1: Genesis, Exodus, Numbers, Joshua
Book 2: Judges, Ruth, 1&2 Samuel, 1 & 2
Kings, 2 Chronicles, Nehemiah, Esther, Job,
Jeremiah, Daniel, Jonah. Judges, Ruth, 1&2
Samuel, 1& 2 Kings, 2 Chronicles; Nehemiah,
Esther, Job, Jeremiah, Daniel, Jonah.

Take the Bible seriously
and have loads of fun while you are at it!

Are you looking to add another dimension to
your teaching? Do you want to encourage your
children to read the Bible? Do you want them
to have strong Biblical foundations without
compromising on fun and activity? TnT have
developed The Game Is Up for this very
purpose. There is a companion volume to this
book: The Game is Up Old Testament Book 1
which covers Genesis, Exodus, Numbers and
Joshua. There are also plans for books on the
New Testament to come out in the following
year.

**All the games are directly linked to the
lessons with strong Biblical emphasis
that covers all major Christian doctrines.
Visual aids for photocopying and clearly
explained teaching points make this an
excellent addition to any church resource
library.**
**Book One covers Genesis, Exodus,
Numbers and Joshua.**
**Book 2 covers Judges, Ruth, 1&2
Samuel, 1 & 2 Kings, 2 Chronicles,
Nehemiah, Esther, Job, Jeremiah,
Daniel, Jonah. Judges, Ruth, 1&2
Samuel, 1& 2 Kings, 2 Chronicles;
Nehemiah, Esther, Job, Jeremiah,
Daniel, Jonah.**

☺The successful On the Way series
continued with extra games and
activities.
☺Book 1: 80 game selections;
☺Book 2: 96 game selections
☺Flexible enough to be used with
any curriculum
☺ Strong Biblical Emphasis
☺Multi age (3-11s)
☺Ideal for Holiday Bible Club;
Vacation Bible School

The On The Way series continues
Book 1: Abraham; Jacob; The Messiah (Christmas)
Jesus said, 'I am...'; Ruth

Book 2: Rescue (Easter); Paul (Acts 9-16 and 17-18)
Philippians; 1 Thessalonians; Suffering

Syllabus for On The Way for 11-14s

Book 1 (28 weeks)	Book 3 (28 weeks)	Book 5 (26 weeks)
Abraham (7) Jacob (7) The Messiah (Christmas) (2) Jesus said, 'I am ...' (7) Ruth (5)	Joseph (7) People in Prayer (7) The Saviour of the World (Christmas) (3) Is God Fair? (Predestination) (2) Learning from a Sermon (3) The Sermon on the Mount (6)	Bible Overview (26)
Book 2 (25 weeks)	**Book 4 (25 weeks)**	**Book 6 (27 weeks)**
Rescue (Easter) (3) Paul (Acts 9-16) (7) Philippians (5) Paul (Acts 17-18) (3) 1 Thessalonians (6) Suffering (1)	Psalms (Easter) (2) Paul's Latter Ministry (7) Colossians (5) Choose Life (Hell & Judgment) (2) The Kings (9)	A Selection of Psalms (5) The Normal Christian Life (7) Revelation (9) Homosexuality (1) The Dark Days of the Judges (5)

The books can be used in any order.

The number in brackets indicates the number of lessons in a series.

For more information about *On the Way for 11-14s* please contact:
Christian Focus Publications, Fearn, Tain, Ross-shire, IV20 1TW / Tel: +44 (0) 1862 871 011 or
TnT Ministries, 29 Buxton Gardens, Acton, London, W3 9LE / Tel: +44 (0) 20 8992 0450

Christian Focus Publications publishes biblically-accurate books for adults and children. If you are looking for quality Bible teaching for children then we have a wide and excellent range of Bible story books - from board books to teenage fiction, we have it covered. You can also try TnT's complete teaching Syllabus for 3-9 year olds; 9-11 year olds as well as the pre-school age group. These children's books are bright, fun and full of biblical truth, an ideal way to help children discover Jesus Christ for themselves. Our aim is to help children find out about God and get them enthusiastic about reading the Bible, now and later in their lives. Find us at our web page: www.christianfocus.com

TnT Ministries

TnT Ministries (which stands for Teaching and Training Ministries) was launched in February 1993 by Christians from a broad variety of denominational backgrounds who were concerned that teaching the Bible to children be taken seriously. The leaders were in charge of the Sunday School of 50 teachers at St Helen's Bishopsgate, an evangelical church in the City of London, for 13 years, during which time a range of Biblical teaching materials was developed. TnT Ministries also runs training days for Sunday School teachers.